Daring to Trust

Daring to Trust

Opening Ourselves to
Real Love and Intimacy

David Richo

SHAMBHALA
Boston & London
2011

Shambhala Publications, Inc.
Horticultural Hall
300 Massachusetts Avenue
Boston, Massachusetts 02115
www.shambhala.com

9 8 7 6 5 4 3

Printed in the United States of America

♾ This edition is printed on acid-free paper that meets the
American National Standards Institute Z39.48 Standard.
♻ This book is printed on 30% postconsumer recycled paper.
For more information please visit www.shambhala.com.

Distributed in the United States by Random House, Inc.,
and in Canada by Random House of Canada Ltd

Designed by James D. Skatges

The Library of Congress catalogues the hardcover edition
of this book as follows:
Richo, David, 1940–
Daring to trust: opening ourselves to real love
and intimacy / David Richo.—1st ed.
p.   cm.
ISBN 978-1-59030-824-0 (hardcover: alk. paper)
ISBN 978-1-59030-924-7 (pbk.: alk. paper)
1. Trust. 2. Love. 3. Intimacy (Psychology) I. Title.
BF575.T7R53 2010
158.2—dc22
2010022881

In affectionate memory
of my caring mother,
Louise,
and
my path-lighting friend
Faye Honey Knopp

I will never forget you

What have we ever,
more or better,
than our life together?

Contents

Introduction

We now embark on a voyage into waters more often troubled than tranquil. Only we bravehearts will want to board the ship called *Trust*. Can we trust the ship not to sink? Can we trust our shipmates? Those are the questions we keep pondering with respect to our families and relationships, not to mention our world.

Only those of us willing to be vulnerable can sail this Sea of Risk. If we fall overboard, headlong into the billows, we may fear their engulfing us. Can we trust our fragile bodies to stay afloat in such a rowdy sea? We tread water with no guarantee that the promised or hoped-for hand will be there for us in the chill and buffeting waves. And will the intrepid mate who dares to swim in our direction get us back on board and stay with us from ship to shore? There are fearsome hazards in the tides of human trust. But these are risks that most of us have been willing to take, again and again, greatly to our credit.

Sometimes our cruises pulled into ports where great loyalty awaited us. For that we were appreciative. Sometimes we have been severely betrayed by the one who seemed to be there for us but was not. For that we grieved. Our history of trust is the ship's log of our life.

What follows in these pages is sometimes a life jacket, sometimes an anchor, sometimes little more than a plank stretching precariously over the lonesome blue uncharted deep. But we will find a way to surf the waves, not drown in them.

How This Book Came to Be

The origin of this book goes back to a memorable moment in a marriage-counseling session I was facilitating with a couple I will call Alice and Eric. Alice had had an affair, now over, and Eric had recently found out about it. Their purpose in therapy was to restore their relationship—that is, to rebuild trust.

The therapy had been making it clear to all of us that it was extremely difficult for Eric to trust his wife again, even though she had voluntarily ended the other relationship and had made a sincere commitment to fidelity and to working things out. Enough time had elapsed so that it did seem reasonable—to all three of us—that Eric could at least *begin* to trust Alice again. But that was not happening, even after some rather intense therapy sessions.

During a particularly poignant moment, Eric was crying and I suddenly realized that his issue was not about trusting Alice. It was bigger than that. It was about his inability to trust anyone fully. Eric's grief in that moment was for all the betrayals in his life from childhood until now. His tears were about how each one had shut him down so that now, when trust was appropriate, he just could not summon it up. The fear that is natural in all grief had, for him, become more like a phobia.

Eric's question was not Is it safe to trust you? His real question was Is it safe to trust anyone?

That one session, a conference of tears, led me to realize more acutely than ever that trust is twofold. Trust can be a response to trustworthiness, but, prior to that, it has to be an ability, gained from experiences of secure relating in our past. Our trust capacity is proportional to the trustworthiness we have found in all our fellow travelers on life's voyage, especially in Mom and Dad. Thus, we are not alone in building our flotation skills on life's tempestuous sea. Trustworthy people in our lives from childhood to the present moment live on in our psyches as accompanying and stabilizing presences. They become part of our inner resources, the psychological and spiritual structures in ourselves that give us power to face threats and deal with our needs. Our memories of trustworthy people and our nostalgia for them are reminders and evocations of these resources. When the trustful bonds were being forged by and with them, our inner resources were being thereby installed. Now when we feel overwhelmed, we have a well of memories to draw strength from. Ralph Waldo Emerson spoke of this encouraging possibility in his address at Harvard Divinity School in 1838: "We mark with light in the memory the few interviews we have had with souls that made our souls wiser, that spoke what we thought, that told us what we knew, that gave us leave to be what we inly are."

I have had many experiences of synchronicity between myself and the clients who choose to see me. Synchronicity is a meaningful coincidence, in which random chance and a personal meaning happen together. It is synchronicity that just the right clients seem to come along to show me something about myself that I am able to see only at that time. In the process of working with a client, I find myself discovering hidden truths within myself, those that had been deep-dungeoned in my past. That turning-point session led me to look at myself and to wonder if I, and maybe many other people, have the same problem that Eric had. I was gripped by the question of how well I completed that first task in life, to become able to trust.

I figured that if all this fascinated me, it was really a calling to explore it and to use what skills I have to write about it. My sights widened to the whole issue of trust, not only fidelity to a partner but faith in every area of life. I realized that I, and so many of us, like Eric, suffer from a sadly wrecked capacity to trust, in ourselves, in people, in reality, or in a power beyond us all. My curiosity and enthusiasm grew, and many realizations began to come to me. I wanted to share them, and that is how this book set off on its maiden voyage.

Some of us trust easily and appropriately because we have had a safe and secure past. Many of us have a somewhat compromised experience of trust since our parents were mostly trustworthy but sometimes failed us. A few of us were so betrayed and abused—traumatized early in life—that we lost our ability to trust at all. Our adult relationships then might seem like one long episode of post-traumatic stress.

Eric was not in that latter category, but he had been disappointed enough, both in childhood and in adulthood, to become extremely cautious about trusting others. Since part of the definition of trust is that it includes taking a risk, extreme caution really means not trusting.

Eric and Alice had never had a conversation about their capacities to trust, a crucial feature of getting to know each other as partners. Part of our work together in therapy was to open up the topic by looking at their earliest and latest experiences of trust and their impact on each of them.

A declaration of our own *history of trust* is essential in understanding ourselves and in growing in intimacy with our partner. We have to name the players in our personal trust story and talk about our experiences with each one. We have to ask ourselves if we fully appreciated each find (each person who proved to be worthy of our trust) and if we fully grieved each loss (each person who let us down). We also ask ourselves if, instead of grieving, we have minimized the impact of our disappointments and abandonments. A breach of trust affects us much more deeply than our cavalier shrug might indicate.

Eric's trust in his relationship with Alice was damaged recently, but his capacity to trust was damaged long ago. Since the difficulty for Eric was not about trust as a *response* to the recent situation but about trust as an overall *capacity,* we placed special attention on his earliest recollections of his parents and how he could or could not trust them. I am reluctant to make one partner "the one with the problem." In this part of the therapy, I said just that and asked permission to work with Eric, in Alice's presence, for a while. For Eric the issue was a damaged capacity to trust. For Alice it was a history of not being trusted—what became our next focus—in Eric's presence.

When a partner is sitting silently in the room where our personal work is being addressed and processed, we feel *accompanied* by her, and intimacy progresses in abundant ways. Within each session, I turned to the other partner and asked how she or he was feeling and what she or he saw in the work the partner did. What a nifty way for one spouse to learn to listen with compassion and for the other to learn to trust—such rich contributions to intimacy.

The work for this couple was so primal, so basic, that it was like starting the whole relationship over again, not just recovering from the recent infidelity. I wondered how many couples are at that ground-floor level and don't realize it.

The therapy started where Alice and Eric wanted to start: mending the breach of trust in the relationship. We all found out that the real starting point was opening the wounded trust from long ago and working toward healing that too.

The opposite of interpersonal trust is not mistrust. It is despair. This is because we have given up on believing that trustworthiness and fulfillment are possible from others. We have lost our hope in our fellow humans. The therapy with Eric made it clear, at a profound level, that he had lived for a long time in despair, something Alice surely must have picked up on over the years but at a level too elusive to be put into words. When all this came to the fore, when we had words for it all, when the feelings gushed out, the couple could mutually develop the capacity to trust and be trustworthy too. What could be more valuable to any of us?

Our Need, Our Fear, Our Risk

Trustworthiness means deserving of trust, which is our first need in life. Perhaps in time it became our worst fear. In the venture of our evolving as adults-in-relationship, it becomes our finest risk.

One of the givens of life is that some people are trustworthy and some are not. Our risk is then to be open to receive loyalty in the moment with appreciation and to deal with later betrayal with grief and without retaliating.

An adult will trust others conditionally—that is, whenever it is wise to do so based on experience. People become trustworthy when the record shows that they are consistent in acting justly, being truthful, and showing loyal love. A spiritually conscious person will unconditionally trust the power of justice, truth, love. We can't always trust that we or others will live in accord with these ideal virtues, but we can trust that they make the world a better place when we do live up to them.

We cannot always trust ourselves, but we can choose to act trustworthily toward others no matter how they act toward us. We can commit ourselves to this and make amends if we fail in it. As we practice unconditional trustworthiness, we notice a healing result: we are no longer devastated when others fail us. Our focus has shifted from ourselves as victims of others' betrayals to fidelity to our own commitment to trustworthiness. We still see that some people are not trustworthy, and we feel sad and injured. But as long as we do not follow suit, we are not so hurt as we once were—and we like ourselves more. This does not mean that we have become naive or gullible. It actually shows that we trust ourselves more. Then we become more discriminating in recognizing trustworthiness in others.

We might summarize by saying: as we become more adult in how we live life, we do not fear trusting others but we do remain on our toes. At the same time, *though we can't trust everyone, anyone can trust us if we are living in integrity.* To use a simple example: At the public pool, I can hand my wallet to only the one person I know and trust while I go for a swim. But any one of the hundred people can trust me to hold his or her wallet.

This book is about how to trust and how to be trustworthy. We will explore trust as a need, fear, and risk. We begin by exploring the meaning of trust and the origins of trust in our emotional lives. Then we look at the four directions our trust can take: toward others, toward ourselves, toward reality, toward a higher power or spiritual path.

Together, you and I will search the cabins of the ship called *Trust* as it sails or founders on the Sea of Risk. We will discover what trust entails, whom to trust, how to rebuild broken trust, how to stop looking for love in hearts that failed us before. We shall come to understand the difference between the way a child trusts and the way an adult trusts.

Most of all, we shall see how every one of our fears is a trust issue. We do not simply fear closeness, commitment, feelings, or giving our heart to someone. Such fears are the wake left by a dark ship called *Fear of Trusting Myself.* Now we will fearlessly catch up with that ship and rechristen it *Ready to Risk.*

> *I put myself out there on the vast and open sea.*
> —ULYSSES TO DANTE IN *THE DIVINE COMEDY*

Practice

EXPLORING OUR HISTORY OF TRUST

Before reading the chapters in this book, you may want to investigate your own history of trust.

List the people whom you have trusted in the course of your life. After each name, write about your experience of trust with that person. Asking yourself questions such as these may help:

How reliable, truthful, and committed was this person to me?

What promises did he or she make to me, and were they kept?

What was I expecting that arose from my own beliefs or projections rather than from an explicit agreement made between him or her and me?

If trust was broken, was this person willing to admit it, make amends, and be open to rebuilding the trust between us?

Did I keep trusting when it was obvious that trustworthiness would not be forthcoming?

Is any of this a pattern?

Did I ever fully grieve for whatever betrayals I experienced so that I could move on with my own life?

Did I act in a trustworthy way no matter how I was treated?
Did I express appreciation for the trustworthiness that was
shown to me?

An exercise like this helps us in a variety of ways: We notice
how our ability to trust people today is influenced by our past.
We recognize patterns in how others relate to us. We see how
our expectations figure into our way of trusting others. We find
clues to our fears of or our limitations in trusting.

It is always possible to grow in trust and to become more
adept at setting boundaries so we are not taken advantage of.
The more we explore, the more we see how our trust in others
is the direct result of our history. Then we can design a style of
relating that is innovative, reality-based, and certainly more
satisfying.

1

What Is Trust?

We might ask why there is a word for trust. It exists in our vocabulary because we know what it is like to mistrust. An opposite helps us notice what we might take for granted. Thus, we would not know others' love if it were not for our experience of indifference. A fish would not have a word for water until it was washed up on the shore.

The *American Heritage Dictionary* defines *trust* as "a firm and hopeful reliance on the fidelity, integrity, or ability of a person or thing." It is not dependency but rather an inner assurance, a confidence that gives us a sense of security. Trust is therefore a *reliance on reliability*. The reliability element, however, is based on our perception or expectation and may not be forthcoming or lasting when push comes to shove. It is in the hands of someone else. Anything beyond our control will always be a source of anxiety and complexity. This suspense is what makes trust such a knotty issue for most of us. In fact, just as pets learn to trust their masters when they notice that they can maintain control, we might presume someone is trustworthy because he is or seems to be in control.

Trust comes from an old Norse word, *traust,* meaning "help or confidence." It is also related to a German word, *trost,* meaning "comfort or consolation." The words denote the sense of certainty that something or someone will come through without fail and that we can be comforted by that assurance. Thus, by definition, we trust others when we can count on their predictable and repeated fidelity, and this makes us feel confident in them for the future. Trust happens in the present and connects past experience with future probability.

We usually use the word *trust* as a noun. This can give the impression that it is a mental reality. Actually, we understand trust better when we use it as a verb. Trust is more truly a process between people, and so it is more appropriate to speak of "trusting" as we describe our ways of relating to one another.

Trust is not a feeling. It begins as a *belief* about the other, based on our own surmise or on the promises made to us. Then, as the evidence mounts that someone is indeed reliable, our trust becomes an ongoing *quality* of the relationship. A sense of safety and security flows from that reliability, though, of course, trust can be damaged at any time. *Safety* refers to an inner sense that no harm will come to us for freely being ourselves in feeling, word and deed. *Security* refers to an inner sense that someone will be there for us. For instance, we trust the government when we believe it can be relied on to keep us safe from harm, guarantee our freedom, and support our well-being throughout our lifespan. We trust others when we feel safe and secure in their presence.

Our insistence that we will spend time only with those with whom we feel safe increases our trust IQ. Over time, we become more adept at telling the difference between a con artist and a straight-up guy. When we feel unsafe with someone and still stay with him, we damage our ability to discern trustworthiness in those we will meet in the future.

We may also trust in the loyalty or honesty of someone we have recently met and about whom we have an intuition but no evidence. Trust can be based on facial and body language, a mien and manner that seem to indicate trustworthiness. Trust in that instance is a social event, something arising between two people, a mirror-imaging of trust and trustworthiness.

Trust can be based on a presumption. We may trust in the outcome of a sports event when there is a favored team and the chances are in our favor. Trust can also be an unqualified confidence, as, for example, certainty about the arrival of a guest who has just confirmed her impending arrival by cell phone.

More often, trusting implies a gamble. Our confidence may be justified or not, in accord with how others choose to act. As adults, we learn that it is up to us to trust or not, based on our assessment of the trustworthiness we have seen and presume will continue in the other person.

Trust in someone means that we no longer have to protect ourselves. We believe we will not be hurt or harmed by the other, at least not deliberately. We trust his or her good intentions, though we know we might be hurt by the way circumstances play out between us. We might say that hurt happens; it's a given of life. Harm is inflicted; it's a choice some people make.

As our relationship deepens, our motivation for desiring that our partner be trustworthy is not to protect ourselves from having to feel the pain of betrayal or loss. As we trust ourselves more securely, as we trust our ability to grieve, we know we can handle that eventuality. Our motivation for wanting a relationship of mutual trust is the cultivation of a more intimate bond between us.

The foundation of adult trust is not "You will never hurt me." It is "I trust myself with whatever you do." We will still be stunned, confused, and grieved by the betrayals of those we trust. But "Please don't ever hurt me" strikes a note of victimization. Within our stronger self, we might realize: people sometimes break promises, turn out differently from what we expected them to be, change their preferences, and so forth. The adult response may sound like this: "I am prepared to deal with disappointment if and when that might happen—hopefully, never. The more invested I am in my own ideas about reality, the more those experiences will feel like victimizations rather than the ups and downs of relating. Actually, I believe that the less I conceptualize things that way, the more likely it is that people will want to stay by me, because they will not feel burdened, consciously or unconsciously, by my projections, judgments, entitlements, or unrealistic expectations."

Projections are personal thoughts, feelings, beliefs, or motivations that we ascribe to or imagine to be in someone else. Projections happen because confusion arises about pledges made to us and whether we can trust their implications. Objective statements have reliable implications. For instance, "You are accepted into our college" certainly implies that we will be listed as students and be able to take classes. An objective statement has the sense of a contract.

The implications of subjective statements, however, do not necessarily represent contracts. We *imagine* that implicit in "I love you" is "I won't leave you." But that is our projection and is not necessarily promised in the original statement. At the same time, it is thoroughly understandable that we want "I love you" to include the implications that reasonable people have come to associate with it. We want reliability, but it is not real without the test of time: "After all these years, you are still here, so your 'I love you' has meant 'I won't leave you.' Now I can reasonably trust that it will continue to mean that." Nonetheless, to presume that a subjective statement includes what we understand it to be about is expectation, not agreement. Adults have noticed that expectations are not valid and that not even agreements are guaranteed to be kept. But it makes sense for us to trust anyway until proved otherwise.

Intelligent Distrust

Trust is certainly our best path, but sane discernment in how we place our trust is crucial too. All of us have been lied to, deceived, duped, or let down in some way. There is no question that trust in humans has to be provisional, given what we see in human behavior. There are some people whom we can trust at first but later they turn on us. Others were fooling us all along, as in a hoax or confidence game.

The con man, the snake-oil salesman, is a perennial character in the story of humanity. He is the predator, part of the trickster archetype. He can readily spot an easy target, a sitting duck, someone who is gullible and naive, the archetype of the innocent victim. The flimflam man violates trust by tricking someone into thinking he is trustworthy when he is the opposite. A "mark" is someone who can be taken advantage of by being so ingenuous, who may also be motivated by greed or a belief that there is a fast track to some promised benefit.

These two archetypes, the trickster and the victim, contradict and undo the relationship of healthy trust between humans. However, developing a spiritual consciousness, as we will see in this book, helps us to avoid both styles. When we practice compassion and integrity, we will never con or trick someone; our commitment is to unconditional trustworthiness. When we act in accord with wisdom, we will let go of unworthy motivations in ourselves and watch out for those who are eager to capitalize on our trusting nature.

Interestingly, the same two styles, conning and swallowing whole, appear between corporation-owned news networks and their viewers. The average person watching the news on television presumes he or she is witnessing the full truth. But often what is reported is the version of or slant on a current event that fits with corporate interests. When we do not check further for our news from less prejudiced or self-interested sources, we are prey rather than well-informed citizens.

Throughout the history of humanity, the more guarded person has survived better than the gullible one. The blithely unwary person may become a victim of deception. However, if, in our ordinary daily routine, we are suspicious of people who are indeed trustworthy, we lose connections with people who really matter to us. Remaining heart-centered while being continually cautious is the safer path when threats and dangers can arise from any quarter.

Some people are unreliable in minor areas but we can definitely trust their love for us. For instance, a friend may be consistently late but we have no doubt about his loyalty. We will then easily make allowances and aim our trust in the direction that matters. This is an example of how we can love someone when our trust in him is limited.

A Latin word for "trust" is *fiducia*. A fiduciary relationship is one between a trustee, a person trusted to act honestly, and a person for whom the trustee acts. A fiduciary relationship is based on confidence in the presumed honesty and follow-through of someone managing things for our benefit. We trust that we are not being conned. For instance, our relationship to our banker presumes he will not knowingly cheat us. The property tax department is trusted not to overcharge us. We presume that the police will protect us, that our food is not poisoned, that a can marked "peas" does not contain corn instead, that other drivers are not out to kill us, that a teller will be honest, that our parents will take care of us, that our partner will be faithful to us.

Yet, we are not naive. We know that any person or organization with power can be corrupt. Every human enterprise is subject to greed or abuse, be it in financial arrangements, delivery of services, government inspection of items such as food, or any area in which there is a fiduciary relationship. We know that corruption and graft can exist in every municipality and organization, no matter how high-minded its purposes. We realize that power often corrupts trustworthiness and creates a moral amnesia in the ones so corrupted. Along these lines, Mark Twain humorously quipped: "No man's life, liberty, or property is safe while the legislature is in session."

This also reminds us that our country was founded on an intelligent distrust of government. Our enlightened founders discovered from their experience with the British king that their fealty to him had to be provisional, conditioned by the extent of his fairness toward his subjects. They also knew that their own independent government by the people had to have built-in protections, human nature being what it is. This was the origin of the system of checks and balances. Each of the three branches of government is obliged to audit and oversee the others, and the voting public does likewise. We might say that anytime people are in the picture, we have to have intelligent distrust, the equivalent of intelligent trust!

If our trust is to remain thus wisely cautious, we will have to perform regular audits of others, of agencies, of products, of services. Yet we cannot audit reality, only acknowledge it and align to it. We cannot audit God, higher power, Buddha-nature. Faith is trusting without auditing, since we have entered a realm of mystery beyond human reckoning or influence.

Self-trust is always to be placed first in our ability to care for ourselves. Auditing those who promote themselves as faithful to us is a way of doing that. Of course, we cannot always trust ourselves either, since denial, mistakes, and projection are favorite pastimes for most of us. Thus, even we need an audit once in a while, which is nothing to be embarrassed about. Hopefully, the practices in this book can serve as self-auditing tools in our self-arraignment!

Our Capacity for Trusting

We may have been gratified to notice that our original trust—in our parents' caring for us—was wisely invested. When we find that our parents—or any person in our early or later life—are trustworthy, we are launched into an assurance that the world and others have what it takes to fulfill us. Our personal experience generalizes into an attitude toward the collective. This is one of the precious qualities of trust, its tendency to spread.

The healthy installation of trust early in life makes us *able* to discern who is trustworthy and who is not. In addition, a healthy capacity to trust is resilient. If we are fooled by someone—as anyone can be—we learn from the experience, and we move on. We are then left with no need to retaliate. People with an entitled ego—that is, with a fixation on self-satisfaction only—engage in retaliation when their desires are not honored. People with a healthy ego try to understand and to reconcile if possible. That resilient style is the true clue that we have moved through our experience in a spiritually conscious way.

However, when we were not given reason to trust our parents, we may lack trust in the wider world. We may then become cynical and pessimistic. In both instances, of trust-worthiness and lack of trustworthiness, we draw conclusions about the world from the evidence provided by our original caregivers. Fortunately, when they proved to be consistently trustworthy, the capacity to trust that was instilled in us remains in us ever after.

Not everyone comes into this world with the same capacity to trust or the same openness to learning trust from his or her caregivers. We can presume that there *are* genetic factors, not yet understood. We certainly cannot underestimate the impact of intrauterine factors on how our capacity to trust may develop. A fetus will be affected, for instance, by maternal stress during pregnancy. This can make our earth-atmosphere rather unsafe for a little one, about to arrive, who has no recourse against the cortisol stress hormone that Mom is generating. Thus, we may each come into the world with a different capacity to trust based on who knows what subtle happenings in the history of our mother's pregnancy or of the inherited factors that influence temperament. Nonetheless, the capacity to trust is always present in some way, and when it is met with attunement and reliability from caring parents, a child can still learn to trust fully.

It can also be true that since we mammals have trusted for many centuries, we may no longer need to have trust "installed" only by our earliest caregivers or our adult partners. It may now be a genetic imprint of our humanity, happening on its own. We can trust our collective inheritance in this case.

There is, in any event, a neurochemical basis for our capacity to trust. Our brains contain a stress-reducing and calming hormone that acts as a neurotransmitter, oxytocin. It is found in the hypothalamus within the midbrain. Oxytocin receptors may not fully activate in our brain if our early life did not include enough closeness and touch by our caregivers. When oxytocin is reduced, we might find it difficult to trust the partner-candidates who appear later in life.

Oxytocin enters the bloodstream through closeness, cuddling, touch, orgasm. It is also released in women during breast-feeding, so that the mother-child connection can happen in a calm atmosphere. Less stress means more safety, comfort, and security, the essential elements of trust that facilitate bonding. For instance, brain scans have identified how areas in the brain that contain oxytocin become activated when we remember the people we love or look at photos of them.

From a physical perspective, the orbitofrontal cortex is crucial to our capacity to handle our emotions, to understand and receive the emotions of others, and to manage the stresses of daily life. Its growth is directly influenced by interactions within a mother-child bond, especially in physical touch. Thus, our original home and community environment as well as the behavior of our primary caregivers have a direct impact on the evolution of structures in our infant brain, structures that are not fully developed for five years. Our emotional and physical relationship with our parents and significant others is a driving force in how we become who we are.

It's important to note that what matters here is how we *experienced* our childhood caregivers. Others may or may not agree with how we perceived things in childhood, but that doesn't matter. The key is how we felt in relationship to our parents rather than some objective measure or standard of the care we received.

Regarding touching, it is central to trusting. Without it we may wonder if someone really cares about us. Many of us are, and have always been, touch-starved. We may have suppressed our needs for contact and communion—which is a form of despair about finding what we need in others. In adulthood we may look to sex as a substitute for the touch and holding we need. Then we use our genitals and those of others to do what hearts are supposed to do.

On the other hand, we may fear touching others. In this way we miss out on the emotional liveliness that makes human relating so exhilarating. As we learn to trust ourselves, putting our arm around someone's shoulder or giving a kindly embrace becomes easier, and it certainly means a lot to the other person. We trust ourselves more—and others trust us more— as we let go of our inappropriate inhibitions. Touch is trust in the form of a hand or kiss.

> *Man, like the gen'rous vine, supported lives;*
> *The strength he gains is from the embrace he gives.*
> —Alexander Pope, *Essay on Man*

Needs and How They Play Out

For most of us, our parents came through reliably with bed and board. They could be trusted to provide a roof over our heads every day of every year. But could they go one day without controlling, criticizing, or belittling us? These were all signs of not trusting us, and this makes it hard later to trust ourselves. We could tell them we had a stomachache, but could we share our gut feelings with them? Our basic survival needs were taken care of, but what about our deeper growth needs?

According to Abraham Maslow, we have a hierarchy of needs. He describes deficiency needs as those based on physical and safety requirements, such as food, shelter, security, and a sense of belonging. These are the needs we have in common with all other mammals. We also have growth needs that serve our higher requirement for self-actualization. The word "deficiency" may minimize our natural needs. Nowadays we see things less dualistically, holistically rather than hierarchically.

We appreciate both sets of needs as equally useful in our development. Our diet, for instance, is no longer simply fuel but makes an important contribution to our psychological and spiritual health too.

In our discussion here, we can see our needs on a spectrum and simply distinguish our immediate survival needs from our deeper emotional needs. Our survival needs are first physical— being clothed, sheltered, and fed. In addition, our survival needs include safety, security, belonging. We need to know that our place in the family is assured, that our parents will not abuse us, that we are protected from danger both at home and in the larger world.

Trust in others develops when children's alarm is met with attunement and protection. When their own mastery of fear and stress makes it possible for them to modulate their feelings, trust in themselves grows too. The need for safety and security from others is essential, but it represents an elementary-level ingredient of our development, fulfillment of a deficiency need. This is why we can say that in early stages of growth, our sense of safety and security comes from others; in full maturity, it becomes our own inner resource, fulfilling our need for growth.

This emotional, higher-growth need—our need for self-actualization—requires being given the time, space, and resources to become who we, as Ralph Waldo Emerson phrased it, "inly are." Our higher needs include making full use of our gifts, finding and fulfilling our calling, being loved and cherished just for ourselves, and being in relationships that honor all of these. Such needs are fulfilled in an atmosphere of the five A's by which love is shown: attention, acceptance, appreciation, affection, and allowing. The quality of allowing is especially important to our growth, making room for us to experience our life fully with no restrictions on the range of our emotions, self-expression, or choices. Allowing is directed into three areas:

1. We are free to show our feelings without being interrupted, punished, or ridiculed for them.
2. We have full permission and encouragement to declare and to live in accord with our own deepest needs, values, and wishes.
3. Our path is smoothed for us by caregivers who protect *and* launch us so we can make our own choices and move out and on when we are ready.

Our survival needs are about ensuring healthy physical development; our emotional needs are about personal growth and evolution. Our survival needs are fulfilled when we are safe at home; our emotional needs are fulfilled when we are valued at home and launched on a voyage too. Our survival needs are about comfort; our emotional needs are about challenge.

We humans are genetically geared for survival. Unfortunately, we are not equally geared to having healthy relationships. So we have to *work* on making intimacy and other growth needs a priority because our body has survival mode as its primary default setting. This explains why we might stay in a relationship that is not working: we imagine that we need it on a survival level. With healthy boundaries, we make a choice for personal happiness and sanity. We then no longer believe we need a relationship in order to survive.

In adult life, the distinction between our survival needs and our emotional needs can apply to two motivations for relationship: We can desire to be in a relationship only for safety and security, our mammalian goals. We can instead be satisfied only with an ongoing committed relationship of intimacy, our human fulfillment.

When we seek safety and security only from someone else without building it in our adult caretaking self, we may come across to others as needy and desperate. When we have safety and security within ourselves and seek intimate connection, we come across as open but not desperate. Our need then is not to be filled, only to be enriched. Henry David Thoreau said it this way: "I will come to you, my friend, when I no longer need you. Then you will find a palace, not an almshouse."

If we missed out on the fulfillment of our emotional needs in childhood and have not worked on that, we may not be ready for adult relating. We may be seeking a relationship in an attempt to correct or replace what was missing in childhood: we may be seeking parenting. Although a partner can act in loco parentis and fulfill that need for us, a partner who is eager to play that role probably has his or her own unresolved childhood issues. Neither partner then is on adult turf. In addition, Eros does not relish the parent-child bond, so he leaves the bedroom quite quickly.

Fortunately, in adulthood we do not need as much safety and security as children do. When we still need safety and security at the child level we may cling to a caretaking partner. We fear losing what only children really need. In a mature relationship, we are equals who give and receive the five A's. In a relationship we use for safety, we are in a dependency relationship with a parental figure. This affects our way of trusting: our trust in the child-parent relationship is unconditional and blind. This keeps us stuck in dependency and makes us likely to stay in relationships that do not help us grow.

Parents are expected to fulfill 100 percent of our needs in early life, including safety and security. As adults, we learn to find need fulfillment in ourselves, in our friends, in our family, in our pets, in our career, in our spiritual program, in nature, and in any other resources we may discover. We then do not rely on a partner, or on any person, for more than 25 percent of our need fulfillment. This includes our need for safety and security.

When we come from a childlike position, we demand more

than that from a partner. This is another way that our emotional needs can feel to us like survival needs. It also helps explain why the ending of a such a strongly needed relationship might lead a partner to consider suicide. The prospect of having our emotional goods suddenly snatched from us makes us feel bereft and empty, since we may have so few resources in ourselves to fall back on. We believe we have nothing going for us without our partner by our side. This makes for an aloneness that feels like the bottom just fell out of our stomach—and our whole life. Sadly, we did not build enough trust in ourselves, since our entire reliance was on the other. Our overemphasis on dependency comes back to bite us when the object of it is gone. No one was meant to live with just one resource. This is why we now feel so dispossessed and cast adrift. Our allowing ourselves to be deluded has left us denuded.

To summarize, we can say that our need for safety and security is part of living in relationship to anyone, but only the survival part. The second and culminating part of our need is for mutual love and personal fulfillment manifested in the form of the five A's (attention, acceptance, appreciation, affection, and allowing). When these were associated with letdown in our original experience of life with others, we will have trouble trusting later. That "trouble" has to be called by name: fear. Our fear in intimate relationships is not of closeness but of the disappointment we imagine will surely follow commitment, since once burned, twice shy. This superstition can be refuted as we accept the fact that though some people hoodwink us, others do not. In any case, we can survive being let down by others— and we can grow in the process.

Our tattered trust history—and the associations that we created because of it—affect us in a long-term way. All the exciting dates that raised our hopes and then were followed by rejection still sit uneasily in our tender hearts. Putting ourselves out there to be battered by disappointment or dismissal takes a toll on us psychologically. That history comes back to haunt us in the form of self-recrimination, a sense of not being good enough to be loved for long. That is a normal reaction in beings such as us, to whom others' opinions and behavior matter, nothing to be ashamed of. As we mature, the opinions will matter less because our own resources have grown beyond them. We have transcended concern about others' opinions. We care about our personal integrity and lovingkindness in how we interact with them.

As we stop taking rebuffs too seriously, we like ourselves more, and that becomes more nurturing than whether someone wants us. Our whole manner changes, and we are, ironically, much more appealing to others, especially to healthier others. Then, look at us, we can even pick and choose a partner rather than wait for someone to ask us to dance.

Only two qualities can get us to that point. The first, as stated above, is building inner resources so that our safety and security lie stably within ourselves. Such inner resources help us look at others with a desire for connection rather than with neediness. The second is our utterly thorough and unconditional yes to the given of human caprice, something we notice now not with horror and blame but with understanding and even amusement.

Reading Ourselves

As a baby, Andrew notices that he has a need to eat and that his caregivers may not always be aware of when this need arises within him, so he cries loudly to be fed. When Andrew feels a need to be held, he uses an altered cry to make this specific need understood. He has to trust that his mother will know that this cry has a different purpose. Andrew's needs rotate between food, holding, and changing of diapers—and he always knows which one is up for him. But his cries require interpretation. After a while, his mother becomes more adept at translating, and Andrew is more confident that his needs can be understood and fulfilled. He has participated in getting his needs met, and this grants Andrew a sense of agency and effectiveness that will keep growing throughout his life, all things being reasonably favorable.

Forty years later, Andrew is divorced and is sitting home alone watching TV, bored and lonely. He will hear a cry from within that he interprets as a need for a snack. In reality, he does not need food; he needs to be held. How incongruous that Andrew has lost the skill of knowing what he really needs and has not yet built the skill of interpreting his longings that his mother learned from him.

In infancy, Andrew believed that his world could be trusted if his need for nurturance was met. His first definition of happiness was responsiveness to and fulfillment of his needs. That gave him a capacity to trust, an important resource. But Andrew did not keep investing in his inner resources, the ones that he might have gained from working on his issues, especially in relationships.

His healthy childhood trust does not protect him now from his own misinterpretation of his needs. To know his needs requires the ongoing work of building self-trust. Andrew does not know where happiness is to be found, so he may keep looking in places that have failed him before. All this is warehoused in the body that snacks late at night and will most likely pay for it with ill health.

Our usual style when we have a need is to notice it and then seek fulfillment of it. Our need for food leads to a trip to the supermarket. Our need for aspirin is followed by a trip to the drugstore. We may use that same sequence regarding our need for emotional goods. For instance, we want unconditional love, so we immediately start looking for the partner whom we can trust to offer it to us.

As an alternative, we can practice a style that helps us know ourselves more deeply. We can first *follow* our need to see what it reveals about us and only after that seek fulfillment of the need, now understood more accurately. A need is then like the White Rabbit that leads Alice down the rabbit hole into Wonderland, the unconscious part of herself where she discovers qualities in herself previously unknown to her. A need can do that for us if *instead of immediately running to someone for fulfillment, we take time to explore it.* Perhaps our need for wholehearted unconditional love shows us what we missed in childhood. Perhaps it is an immature striving based on a sense of entitlement, a case of ego at the helm. Perhaps it is a lack of loving ourselves enough. The following practice helps us *know ourselves through our needs.*

Practice

FOLLOWING OUR NEEDS

In this and in all our practices, we have to change only one small thing in our lives and we contribute to our growth. That helps us trust ourselves more. By success in small areas of life-renewal, with baby steps outside our usual and negative patterns, we train ourselves for bigger challenges and our trust in ourselves grows accordingly. This is because we realize that we are putting energy into what helps us. Now we trust ourselves as devoted caretakers of ourselves.

This practice is simple: we notice our need, follow it, and only then seek to fulfill it, in perhaps a new way. Now we are reading our needs and using them as resources for self-knowledge. We are finding out that what we want tells us something meaningful about ourselves. That can become more fascinating to us than the jump to immediate fulfillment. With this practice, we may discover a new need or a more exact one, which gives us deeper appreciation of ourselves.

(Here *deeper* and *depth* refer to a mysterious reality behind all beings, events, and appearances that is meaningful and valuable. We know ourselves deeply when we trust that we have an enlightened nature always underlying our choices and behavior, no matter how unenlightened they may seem. Depth in this sense, by the way, is what is meant by the spiritual dimension of an experience or of reality.)

To read your needs, ask yourself the questions below. (Some people find it helpful to write out their answers in a journal or on a computer.)

1. What am I feeling a need for in this moment?
2. What am I afraid will happen if I do not fulfill this need?
3. What is the story I am telling myself about having this need? For example: "I am wrong [or right] to want this." "I am inadequate, so I will not be able to find fulfillment." "I do [or do not] deserve to be fulfilled." "I am entitled to this." "Having this will make me happy forever."
4. How is this need familiar, especially from childhood?
5. What messages have I received about having a need like this before, especially from my parents?
6. What are other possible reasons for my present need?
7. How does this need connect with my other needs?
8. How intense is this need, and what is that telling me about myself?
9. Has my usual way of fulfilling this need been successful?
10. Do I have it in me to be satisfied at this time?
11. Is this what I really want, or is this a substitute for a deeper need?
12. How can I fulfill that need?

To summarize the practice, we move from this model of need fulfillment:

> Feel the need. → Fulfill the need literally,
> as I first named it.

To this model:

> Feel the need. → Follow the need to its deeper meaning. → Fulfill the need in that new way.

This practice helps us trust our needs.

Extra-Credit Assignment—Following this practice and all the practices you do in this book, write a poem that expresses what you have discovered about yourself. When you finish reading the book, assemble all your poems as a pamphlet with a title of your choice. Save this as a reminder of the work you are doing on yourself. Copy and share your book of poems with the people in your life whom you trust. What better gift than this record of your progress in trusting and trustworthiness?

There Are Healthy Connections

Psychoanalyst Erik Erikson described human psychological development as a series of conflicts or challenges, each of which must be resolved before we can move up to the next level of our growth and development. He defined the first developmental conflict as trust versus mistrust, and it occurs in infancy. Our later challenges require a satisfactory resolution of the trust issue before they can be successfully negotiated. Only as people who become able to trust can we proceed along the path to a healthy, fulfilled life. This is because trust is the foundation of all human connections.

If we missed out on trust in early life, we need not despair. We may find people who are consistently trustworthy toward us later in life. Such relationships can be corrective and complementary. They provide us with a new opportunity to learn to trust if our trust was injured, lost, or missing in childhood. When we open to others, take the risk of trusting, and are not disappointed, we are, in effect, newly parented. Then the trust that was lacking in childhood is finally installed in us. Intimacy with another adult has become a path to wholeness for us.

Neurologically, this can mean that we are restoring or rebuilding our neural networks for trust. Scientists have shown that our brain has a lifelong plasticity, or changeability. We have a lot going for us: our inherent nature is ever open to evolving into the best version of itself. We can trust that when we take the psychological steps, neural shifts will occur. Our inner self wants to be healthy and joins us in the exuberant momentum that leads us to wholeness and healing. In any case, early life experiences do not determine our future but only influence it, so we always have yet another chance at health and happiness.

Another chance means that though our original experience forms the basis of our personality, we have the capacity to step back from negative patterns and work with them. We can address, process, resolve, and integrate the pain and dysfunction of our past.

To *address* means to reflect upon, appraise, and challenge our beliefs about an experience. We then *process* our experience—that is, feel the feelings that arise and notice how they connect to our past. Then we can move toward *resolving* our issue. This means no longer being held up in our move toward relating with others. We then *integrate* our work into our lifestyle. We do this when we take the necessary but risky steps toward trusting others without being stopped or driven by fears that restrained us in the past.

This book often recommends that we address, process, re-solve, and integrate our feelings and experiences. It is impor-tant to be aware that the addressing is also a way of *staying with our feeling, abiding in our experience.* This is a mindful style of focusing on the here-and-now reality rather than our mind's embroideries around it. We will fully address in our-selves only what we fully and compassionately accept about ourselves. Only then do we open to what is going on, and only then do we enter it fully. Most of us do not love ourselves enough to engage in this kind of addressing. We may fear our own truth. As we practice addressing our issues in a mindful and compassionate way, a fearlessness about ourselves devel-ops and we are no longer threatened by the demons inside us, no matter how loudly they growl. This becomes a first step toward trusting others.

With trust, we are no longer caught in the default setting of cortisol-animated stress, with its resulting primitive fears of closeness. We are no longer faced with only the primitive op-tions of "run for cover" or "fight it out." Now we have the op-portunity to take cover in the other and join her in a trusting bond. This is the neural blueprint for psychological change, a reprogramming from stress to safety. The secure trustworthi-ness we have found installs our new ability to trust. What hope we can feel about relationship when we notice a rewiring of what has so long been unconsciously patterned. That kind of trust makes our love for someone real and lasting.

For a long time our fear might have been our only way of knowing we were still alive. Now love becomes the way.

Bonds of Attaching and Relating

Attachment theory describes how security and insecurity in our relationships are connected to childhood. The theory originated with psychiatrist John Bowlby and was further developed by psychologist Mary Ainsworth and then by other contributors. A cursory, and hopefully simplified, explanation of their concepts can help us understand more about the origins and meanings of trust.

Attachment theory basically states that children psychologically attach to those who care for them in order to find safety and security. The innate biological drive to seek closeness to a caregiver when we believe we are in danger activates attachment—that is, bonding in both the child and the caregiver. The quality of safety, comfort, protection, and security that is offered to the infant influences the level of trust that develops in her for the rest of her life. These ideas have been expanded in recent years to include adult relating also.

Attachment, in psychology, refers to our natural desire for physical and emotional closeness to another person. It happens through engaging with one another and responding to one another. Attachment does not mean possessiveness or control but rather engagement and responsiveness by showing the five A's. It is not compulsive clinging, with obsessive thoughts and a gnawing insatiability. Those are the three elements that signal addiction in the psychological realm. They are also what define suffering in the Buddhist teaching on attachment.

Healthy relating happens when we hold gently rather than hang on to someone for dear life, when we keep someone in our hearts without becoming fixated, and when we can be satisfied with reasonable contact rather than feel we can't get enough. The resultant sense of liberation from neediness is worth more than the fulfillment of any need.

By the end of her first year, an infant has learned to maintain her bond to her caregiver by a tried-and-true repertoire of engagement and responsiveness. She can successfully complain when mother leaves the room, display fetching smiles upon her return, cling to mother when she is afraid. A toddler's staying close to familiar people grants her a sense of safety if danger should arise.

To attachment theorists, crying is an innate strategy by an infant to alert a caregiver to his needs. It is also a technique the infant uses to develop his sense of security—an indicator of the value of expressing grief openly all through life. Consistent responses by parents foster secure attachment, and this increases the child's autonomy. The result is less crying and more activation of his powers to self-regulate—that is, self-soothe and modulate feelings in times of stress. This is what leads to self-trust so that safety and security begin to grow within oneself.

We also gain knowledge about how to self-soothe and regulate our feelings through our bonding with others who calmly mirror and confirm them. When there was no such attuning to our feelings, we may be possessed by them or block them. We will find it difficult to stay with our feelings, to address, process, and resolve them. This is because we missed out on the allowing of them. In any case, attunement has to happen only usually, not constantly, for us to learn to trust. It would take a mind reader to attune to our every need and feeling. In any family or relationship, attunement and mirroring happen in moments, and moments are enough.

Specific indicators of attachment bonds change as we grow toward adulthood. For example, a toddler may cry when his mother leaves the room, but a nine-year-old simply shouts, "When will you be back?" A teenager may say nothing, cherish the time alone, and notice if mother comes home later than expected. The preceding two examples presuppose a secure attachment. Children who are anxious about their relationship to their caregivers cannot handle comings and goings so easily.

Mary Ainsworth closely observed children's first year. Her studies pointed to three attachment patterns in children toward their caregivers: secure, anxious-avoidant (insecure), and anxious-ambivalent or resistant (insecure). Here are examples of how these childhood models of attachment show up in adult relating:

Children who were *securely attached* will usually have high self-esteem and an optimistic view of themselves, others, and relationships in adult life. They feel at ease with closeness and do not fear it as a threat to their independence. They are able to balance closeness and distance in how they relate to partners. People who felt secure in childhood have gained stability. This quality makes it possible to state their needs and to ask for resources of fulfillment from others, two requisites for intimacy. Such securely attached persons will be attracted to partners who are themselves stable and equally high in self-esteem. They will not often be driven by a competitive ego that demands supremacy but by a cooperative ego that respects equality. This is because they trust themselves, and that makes it easier for them to trust others. In relationships, they are more likely to be focused on coming to a meeting of minds rather than achieving victory by self-assertion.

Anxious-ambivalent children seek constant assurance, approval, and attention from their caregivers, and then as adults, they may demand this from partners. They may cling to others and come across as excessively dependent. They are more pessimistic about themselves and others and cannot easily trust themselves. They also find it hard to trust others because they believe they are unworthy of meriting enduring love from them.

Anxious-avoidant children are compulsively independent. As adults, they may continue that style. They see themselves as self-reliant and give the impression of not needing close bonds with others. They often conceal their authentic feelings. If someone rejects them, they simply absent themselves, making the resolution of issues in the relationship impossible. If their partner clings, they become distant or aggressive, being quite alert to what feels like engulfment.

In addition, there is the category of the *disorganized* person. This person can focus neither on self nor on other because the original experience of engaging and responding was threatening and bizarre. In childhood, he felt fright with no remedy possible, a style not sustainable for long. As a result, a disorganized person becomes fragmented easily. He can fall apart in stressful situations since he lacks the resilience and equanimity that come from security.

Securely attached children become easily socialized and may be popular among their peers. They are usually empathic and able to care about others. They show independent initiative and an interest in exploring. They are not dependent but can be interdependent. They are not likely to bully or to tolerate being bullied. Bullies have been shown to be mostly anxious-avoidant types, while victims are anxious-ambivalent types.

The narcissistic personality style corresponds to the avoidant attachment style (overfocus on self, not on other; flight response). The borderline personality style corresponds to the ambivalent attachment style (overfocus on other, not self; fight response). When we collapse in crisis, we fall into the paralysis of disorganized attachment (fragmentation, dissociation, freeze response).

The attachment theorists' work validates that an inability to trust is related to deficits in our early bonding experience. These are embedded in our neural circuitry well before we are conscious. Thus, our fear of trusting has a "no-fault" quality. As we mature, we notice our deficits and how they inhibit our chances at healthy intimacy. Then we can take responsibility to heal. This requires grieving our damaged origins without holding anything against our parents now. Our focus is on recovery, not retaliation.

The attachment theory fosters compassion in us. Seeing how trust and trustworthiness are directly related to what happened to us in early life, we realize that no one is the cause of his own trust issues. This can make us more kindhearted toward ourselves for the way we are and toward others for the way they are. No one asked for the hand he was dealt, so everyone deserves compassionate understanding—while we remain responsible for working on ourselves now.

An original secure attachment is the basis of trust. Feeling that we are lovingly held with the five A's, that holes in trust can be darned, that safety and security are reliably present—all these build our confidence in others. Our trust is also in ourselves as people who are now capable both of showing trusting love and of being willing to work on repairing ruptures in fidelity. In the midst of all this, we remain aware of the given that safety and security are nonetheless sometimes absent in people, nature, events, and powers beyond them.

Nevertheless, from our trust in relationships we become able to build a core trust in the universe and its givens, no matter how heavily they land on us. Once our fear of trusting relents, our daring trust becomes a source of equanimity in the face of all that people and events can line up for us. Then we say, "I can handle this hit. It does not have to be a mortal blow."

Practices

BREATHE, PAUSE, START OVER

We now see that trust is directly related to serenity. As we calm down, we can access self-trust. The calming happens by taking deep breaths and by pausing before acting. This is not only breathing but imagining our breaths coming from an utter openness, from our enlightened nature. We also picture our breathing in as an opening of ourselves to receiving from the world and our breathing out as an opening of the world to receiving us. Deep breathing, slowing down, and pausing are features of ritual, showing that they have been perennially associated with spiritual growth.

This technique is not only a way of building trust in ourselves. It is also useful in reestablishing communication when we are caught in dramatic, stressful scenarios with a partner. We can rebuild trust in each other by our three-step practice: breathe, pause, start over calmly. Practice this program on a daily basis, both personally and in your relationships, to prepare for the times when you will need it.

Ordinarily, we do not find it necessary to focus on our breathing because it happens automatically. When we practice focusing on it, we bring consciousness to what is unconscious—and it is a new consciousness. This is especially valuable because it engenders both a habit of self-monitoring and renewal of our inner resources. We are then gaining exponentially because we are laying down neural pathways that increase our consciousness overall.

EXPLORING OUR CHILDLIKE AND ADULT TRUST

Our earliest needs may remain present—and sometimes urgent—throughout our life span. We might expect in a relationship that our partner should fulfill our five-year-old need to be held. But when we meet up with what is required of *us* in an adult relationship, we may be at a loss or feel put upon. Our work then is to redesign our childlike need for holding to fit the style of an adult relationship: We notice and respond to the need in our partner to be held by us. We still desire to be held, but we realize that our partner can't necessarily hold us every time we need it. We find alternative healthy means to fulfill that need.

Study the following chart to notice where you stand at the moment. Do you find yourself in one column or partially in both?

My Childlike Trust Requires:	*When I Have Adult Trust, I Appreciate:*
Absolute reliability and predictability	Reliability when it is offered
Safety and security in a safe haven—for example, within family or relationship	Safety and security in the safe base of myself and, when appropriate, in others too
Soothing and comfort, especially in distress or when I request it	The importance of self-soothing as well as receiving comfort from others when it is offered
Someone who will not betray me, be disloyal to me, or disappoint my expectations	That people sometimes betray, disappoint, and hurt, so it is important to build a personality resilient enough to cope flexibly with all that and to cultivate a spiritual consciousness mature enough not to retaliate (while also being able to say "Ouch!")
Someone who will never leave me	That allowing others to go when they need to is a form of love and does not have to devastate me, except possibly temporarily
Someone who will never hurt me	That being hurt by others and my own vulnerability to it are part of any intimate bond, but I will not tolerate being deliberately or maliciously harmed in any relationship

Someone who will come through for me, stand by and up for me, and be there for me every time I ask	When others come through, stand by and up for me, and are there for me but know that all those are gifts either given voluntarily by them or in response to my request
Someone to give me what my parents may have failed to provide	The importance of grieving what I missed in the past and of not substituting partners for parents
These are fear-based and in childhood are appropriate ways to form secure attachments but in adulthood imply a sense of entitlement.	*These are courage-based and flow from an unconditional yes to people as they are.*

In the falling-in-love state, we may all be in the childlike column, but as we mature within a relationship, we move to the style in the adult column. Did this happen for you?

As you continue in the next chapters, what you will learn and practice will help you in your journey from the childlike column to the adult column.

Finally, use this summary of how trust works in an adult life as your personal checklist:

☐ I trust myself to receive the trustworthiness of others.

☐ I trust myself to handle betrayal by others without being vindictive.

☐ I base my trust on my own intuition and on what the record shows about each person, not on promises or wishful thinking.

☐ I commit myself to being unconditionally trustworthy toward others no matter how anyone ever acts toward me.

☐ Now I see that to be trustworthy does not mean that I have to be rigidly reliable but only reliably real.

We are, in a sense, our own parents and we give birth to ourselves by our own free choice of what is good.
—SAINT GREGORY OF NYSSA,
HOMILY ON THE BOOK OF ECCLESIASTES

2

Our Early Sense of Trust

THE MORE OUR PARENTS attuned to us and validated our emotions, the more we gained a capacity to trust ourselves and the world around us. Attunement is a communing; hence, it is reassuring and confirming. Authentic attunement provides us with a holding environment in which we can feel secure and can trust those who love us. Our trust grows not only from being held when we needed it but also from being let go of when we needed that. The parent who truly attunes to us will hold us but only for as long as we want to be held. Later in life that balance will be the hallmark of successful intimacy.

The opposite of attunement to us is indifference or abandonment. If that happened to us, it becomes difficult later to trust others. If we began to feel that we could not be loved for who we were but only for how well we lived up to what our parents required us to be, we may not trust ourselves. The love that has strings attached does not register in us as love at all but as reward for meeting expectations. We may wonder if we are lovable just as we are. That nagging question in our minds is what edges out self-esteem and, with it, self-trust.

If a parent abused us, it will be hard to trust others *and* hard to trust ourselves. Our bodies are poised for a slap from others rather than a hug. We might have made family abuse bearable by imagining that we were being justly punished for our misdeeds. Though this leads to guilt, the guilt is not as terrifying as believing a parent may have been a bad person and that we may indeed have been orphans. The archetype of the victim maintains some sense of connection, albeit to a persecutor; the archetype of the orphan leaves us with no one.

A cooperative, mutually beneficial relationship with our early caregivers works best. In a healthy family experience, a symbiotic phase of development occurs. This refers to the mutual satisfaction of the need in mother and infant for each other's presence. It peaks when the infant is about five months old. Our first experience of trust is in the containing safety of the mother-child bond. This security equips us for the next phase of growth, that of mobility—crawling, walking—an exhilarating move toward autonomy.

If, within the symbiosis, the mother is so needy that she cannot permit a child's safe transit to more independence, she may resent or fear that developmental move. Such a mother has been unable to give the "A" of allowing. The child of that mother cannot go on to a phase that is not safe, so she lags behind in the one that she is in. This may show itself in a retardation in motility or speech. Baby thereby preserves the comfort of an unconditional symbiotic oneness. But the comfort in that choice feels misaligned because her body/mind is geared to move on.

Symbiosis and autonomy refer to intrapsychic events. They are not meant to be taken literally. They are metaphors for the reality of our mysterious yearning to grow and how it is fulfilled.

In fact, all our psychological and spiritual concepts are metaphors in that same way. We know we are mature in any of our beliefs, psychological or religious, when we appreciate that.

Deep in our primal unconscious, the desire for symbolic total immersion is always vying with our drive toward mobility. The container archetype is battling the journey archetype. When we are at the mercy of what feel like inner contradictions, it is hard to trust ourselves. No wonder we are so very careful about trusting others, so rueful when they fail us.

The origin of our capacity to trust is related to comfort and challenge, the two requirements of growth in all of nature. Baby birds keep warm under the comforting breast of mother and then are challenged when she nudges them out of the nest.

Our development requires a series of similar weaning experiences. We are comforted by the breast but have to accept the challenge of drinking from a bottle and then from a glass, each a move away from contact with Mother and her warmth.

We begin life comfortably at home with mother but then find ourselves at school, with its challenges to cooperate with others. We also face the challenge of being one of many, no longer the one-and-only we were at home. Each move is in the direction of more independence and more interdependence. Each evokes feelings and presents stresses. But we keep noticing that we are innately equipped for what we have to face. Then new comforts emerge from each challenge.

Comforting moments of holding in childhood are stored in our bodies all our lives. They become resources for us in times of loneliness or despair; they remind us that we did not miss out on the best of all human experiences. When someone comes along who triggers or replicates those moments, we feel the original love again and we can then renew our resources. It can happen in an intimate relationship, in therapy, in friendship. When we meet up with genuine trustworthiness in someone, we realize that superficial or ersatz trustworthiness was really only a parody of the real thing. Once we find what is real, we will never settle for less later on.

Here is a personal example of the sense of being held. When I was a small child, my bath was administered every Saturday night in a soapstone sink in Grandma's kitchen, which was downstairs in our tenement house. The sink had a slanted side for washing clothes by hand, so it was a cramped space, but the hot water felt good, especially in winter. The bathing project was performed by my mother, my grandmother, and my great-aunt. Each would work on a different sector of my skinny anatomy (with my genitals left to me). Then they would wrap me in freshly laundered towels, and all of them would dry me off, dust me with baby powder, put me in clean pajamas, and set me by the stove while they made coffee for themselves and warm milk for me. The aromas were complemented by the fragrance of orange and tangerine peels slowly roasting on the cast-iron kerosene stove to give the house a pleasant scent. I dearly treasure this memory of comfort, of being cherished and loved. I can recall it in every detail, and I can still summon up a felt sense of the caring and safety in it. *These are now qualities within me, physically felt, preserved and triggered by a similar experience.* This is what is meant by inner resources.

In adult life, I consulted a female chiropractor who, I was happy to find, worked with a staff of helpers. As I lay on the table, she did adjustments while a second woman massaged me and a third woman placed heating devices on various parts of me. This was pure heaven, not only because of the attentions from the three females but also because it was a replay of the comfort that every cell in my body remembered and now felt again in a living, concrete way. They were not loving me as my relatives did, but I *felt loved* because of the original association of caring touch and genuine affection from my childhood experience.

I carry that sense of being loved today, and it makes it easier to face whatever happens to me. I know without a doubt that the three graces are always surrounding me. The real people are gone, but they live on as inner resources. What was material and external is now internal. What came from others now comes from within me. The love they showed me did not hold me back there with them, tying me to that sink and stove, but gave me a strength to go on to what came next. Is this not the essence of our human journey?

Our First Steps

All through life, we are happiest when we can go anywhere at any time from a nest that is open—one that allows us to take flight and is always ready to welcome us back. In this section, we'll also see that the ways a toddler advances in his development mirror our adult relating. As healthy toddlers (one and a half to two years old), we follow Mother around to maintain our connection to her while we also move off on our own. This behavior combines the twofold desire for independence and for not deserting the one who loves us, a skillful style throughout our lives. At first our mother was crucial in maintaining a symbiosis with us. Then she becomes the secure base we can leave and come back to, a safe haven when needed. The stages of trust shape up this way:

1. I am one with you.
2. I can leave you for a while.
3. I can come back and you will be there.

In the first stage, we need to trust that Mother is always with us. For the second stage, we need to trust that Mother will allow us to go and be there when we need her. We trust at first that

Mother will not let us go, then that she will. She holds and then she lets go—the phases we encounter in adult intimacy too: In romantic attachment, we are symbiotic. Then, in ongoing relating, we trust that we can each go to our own interests—career, hobbies, and so forth—and the other will be there for us when we come back. This is another example of trust and its contribution to both personal fulfillment and intimate relating.

Healthy toddlers come to realize that mothers have other occupations than just gratifying their needs. This is the next challenge for toddlers: to let their sense of entitlement and primary status diminish, another tool for relating to others throughout life. If they are ever to launch out on their own— that is, fulfill themselves—toddlers will have to give up the expectation of being followed and held whenever they demand it. They will notice they can go on with their own life without constant reassurance, another tool for a healthy adult future.

A major change in a toddler's relationship to Mother happens when life is no longer entirely soothing because Mother is now saying no. Comfort has yielded to challenge. This happens as baby is becoming more independent—crawling, then walking. Here is another example of the exquisite synchronicity built into human development. We continually embrace more challenges to be independent just as we have to become less dependent on others anyway.

There is also, however, a connection in the toddler's mind between independence and loss of total approval. The "no" from the one who was at our beck and call before stirs up a crucial trust issue. The challenge is to go on trusting the one who does not jump to satisfy our every need, the one who may question whether our immediate want is legitimate. This will also be an important skill in the toolbox for relationships later in life.

A smooth transition occurs for baby when the bond with Mother feels trustworthy and undisturbed. Then the love behind the "no" is never doubted, important for security; and the boundaries remain in place and consistent, important for safety. This combination of love and respect for relationship boundaries will help us find a balance of wisdom and compassion in how we respond to one another's needs throughout our life span. This is what I call sane affection.

The toddler continues to picture his mother as a home base, but by fifteen months, he recognizes her as a person in her own right. Now the toddler wants to share his world with her. He places objects he has discovered into her lap with pride and with the expectation that his sense of wonder will be mirrored. "Join me in my joy" is an early pathway to trusting that others will understand us and share in our world. This too lays the groundwork for a capacity for intimate sharing later with other adults. We will grow in trust for the partner who mirrors us and feel disconnected from the one who does not.

As toddlers, we idealize our parents. Gradually, our awe becomes more realistic, and we admire them while noticing their faults. This transition from idealizing to reality-based love is how we learn to accept our adult partners as they are. It is also how we learn to deal with disappointments in our relationships. The letdowns do not have to end our bond, only reorganize it around new, more realistic expectations. Realism then balances romanticism.

Trust is sometimes placed in someone *because* we admire him, which is not an appropriate reason. If we put a person on a pedestal and later notice his clay feet, our disappointment is doubled by that realization joined to the breakdown of trust. It is especially distressing when the person we admired and trusted takes advantage of us or abuses us. If such a hurt happened in our childhood, we will feel the pain, but the full felt sense of the loss does not usually kick in until adulthood. Only when our brain can accommodate the full brunt of a loss can our body allow the full grief. Our sobs, eventually, show the authentic feeling that was waiting for us. We won't die from that pain, only know ourselves better and be glad it all came out at last.

To summarize the connection between early developmental tasks and adult intimacy, we can notice how the phases are similar: We are symbiotically connected when we fall in love with each other. We then launch out into the world to do our separate work, but we don't go too far away from each other. Gradually, we realize, especially when a child enters our life, that we are not entitled to constant attention but have to yield that rank to the new arrival or to any other focus that has become important to our partner. Our admiration becomes realistic, and we learn to accept that disappointment from others is part of life and does not have to put an end to the receiving of love or the showing of it. Finally, we appreciate how our feelings are being mirrored, and we offer the same in return.

Fathers are also crucial to our development in early life. Generally, mothers comfort us in the holding environment, and fathers bring us out into the world. Mothers hold us in the container of safety. Fathers show us a path from which to take our challenging journey. They do this when they keep bringing us out into the world of art, sports, work, and nature. Of course, the roles can be reversed or be common to both parents. All that matters is that we have the experience of both the container of coziness and the push into exploration. The containing prepares us to trust closeness in human relations; the launch into exploration helps us trust that our freedom will not thereby be curtailed.

In many families, children notice that Mom complains that Dad is not fulfilling her needs. We may hear this with an implication that he cannot fulfill them. This can lead to ongoing doubts about trusting Dad. It can also mean that boys come to doubt their capacity to satisfy women. Girls may doubt men's capacity to satisfy them. If this happened to us, the work is to separate ourselves from the model of relationship we saw in childhood and to design our own healthier ways of being in relationship. It is not an easy task, but making the connection between past and present helps us get on track.

Traditionally, the container archetype is considered feminine and the journey archetype masculine. We see the distinction palpably in how men and women hold babies. Men walk around and show them things. They look together at the outside world. As adults communicating with other men, they will most likely sit together but be looking outside. Women are more likely simply to hold and cuddle babies while looking directly into their eyes. That same face-to-face style will mostly characterize female-to-female conversations later in life.

In fact, in face-to-face interactions, our mirror neurons are more likely to be activated. Mirror neurons in the brain make it possible to resonate with and imitate someone's behavior or feelings. We will feel empathy when we see the tears in someone's eyes. Our attentive presence with the five A's makes us more likely to feel compassion in a deep way. It also confirms that we have no separate self but are interconnected because, let's face it, who we are changes when other humans are around.

In addition, our mirror neurons may move us bodily. This is because feelings do not occur without a consonant bodily behavior—for example, sadness leads to crying; fear leads to fleeing or fighting. So when we feel with someone, we do not stop there, we put an arm around her. We move toward her in some action meant to show our support through touch.

Our trust capacity is healthily formed in childhood when the comfort from our parents does not feel like smothering and their push does not feel like dismissal. As a result, later in life we can allow closeness and remain independent at the same time. It's not an either/or but a both/and, the bookends of psychological health.

We notice, in all our examples in this section, that our capacity for trust is enlarged by meeting up with reliability in others. It is trust that beats a path to every one of life's goalposts.

It is useful to keep in mind, however, that we can be lulled by reliability. Safety and security, especially in childhood within a family or religion, can feel so important to our survival that we hide our real feelings or our real self in order to ensure their continuance. A child may notice that one or all of his inborn qualities, such as his psychological type (introvert versus extrovert), gender, sexual orientation, or creativity, are not welcome. Preserving his safety and security then becomes more valuable than showing—or even knowing—who he is. This is how seductive and self-negating safety and security can be and why they eventually have to be found within if full personal evolution is ever to happen.

In the final analysis, children dare to be themselves when they trust their parents so much that they can say, "Here I am permitted to be myself. Here it is always acceptable to feel what I feel and to need what I need. Here there is no danger in developing along the lines of my own inner leanings. I am truly free to explore my world and my place in it. Here I have the right to have power and to make the personal choices that reflect my own most cherished values and wishes." Such a declaration by a developing child is a tribute to her parents' ability to accept and allow. This is how an ability of our parents launches our abilities. The activation of their capacity paves the way to the activation of our capacity.

The healthy, autonomous way of living will prove perilous in a world in which we are meant to toe the line, not rock the boat, fit in if we are to succeed. Noticing and cherishing our own uniqueness then leads to feeling isolated. But we can still refuse to be artificial or put on the face that will please others.

And when we dare to be like that, we notice that we attract those, and even that special someone, who can join us in the precarious but splendid enterprise of becoming real.

Gone but Here

The movement and exploration a toddler experiences in Mother's absence springs him from sorrow about his loss into joy about his newfound powers. This joy-while-alone is ever after an antidote to fear of abandonment to those who have committed themselves to moving onward along the adult journey of discovery. Movement, our launching ourselves into going on, is the opposite of loneliness.

Our developmental task as toddlers is to go on exploring while holding the memory of our absent mother. We find our comfort in that *inner* image. We also notice that she is herself motivated and even enthusiastic about coming back to us. In this way, we realize that a bond endures in absence. Later in life this will mean not abandoning our love object for a substitute but waiting for her return. Patience builds trust in ourselves and others both in childhood and in adulthood.

Our trusting that Mother's relationship to us transcends what can be demonstrated only by physical presence is the origin of an exquisite skill that will serve us all through life: Our sense of presence does not have to mean literal physical attendance. It can be felt and imagined in absence; it transcends here-and-now tangible reality. This will apply to faith in the divine, belief that in silence is nonetheless presence.

A sense of presence in absence is a combination of opposites, an experience of paradox that builds our creative imagination. As we grow, we will continually seek figures symbolic of our original nurturance, facsimiles of our caregivers. A personal God might be used as a new safe base or as a prosthetic device for what was given by or what was missing from Mother and Father.

When we received nurturance in childhood, we more easily give it in adult life because we identify with our giver/parent. Safety and security are nurtured by being soothed by someone when we are confused or afraid. To become self-soothing as adults, we need to have received soothing from others. Our capacity is engendered by receiving from others. This helps us go beyond self-soothing to trust others for comfort too. Thus, we move *from trusting in the trustworthiness of someone to trusting ourselves and then to trusting others.* This may also evolve into trusting a higher power.

At the same time, for healthy emotional development, we also need some experiences of frustration. The frustration is optimal for growth when it is a challenge we can handle and for which trusty help is given to us if needed. It is contrary to growth if it remains simply an obstacle and we are shamed for not dealing with it. If too much soothing and protectiveness came our way, we may not have learned to look for need fulfillment within ourselves. We may not trust ourselves because we never had the opportunity to deal with frustration successfully, the very way we learn that we have reliable powers—that is, resources within.

Practices

RECEIVING COMFORT AND FACING CHALLENGE

This chart helps us see how comfort and challenge work together throughout our life span. Where do you place yourself in each decade of your life? Where do you hope or expect to be in the decade to come?

An Accent on Comfort	*An Accent on Challenges*
Leads us to trust in others	Leads us to trust in ourselves
Focuses us on finding a home base	Helps us risk moving toward new horizons,
Happens within the householder archetype	Animates the journey archetype
Focuses us on grounding ourselves	Leads us to stretch ourselves
Makes us cherish security	Forces us to relinquish security
Finds creativity in maintaining and nurturing our home base and those in it	Finds creativity in curiosity and invention
Makes us more apt to hold on	Launches us to move on
Leads us to surrender to the rules in our home environment	Leads us to surrender to the moment
Leads us to stay close to another	Leads us to focus on our personal goal with or without the presence of another
The message to us is: "Don't go too far," or "Don't go."	*Our inclination is: "Go as far as you can."*

TRUSTING AND LOVING

What in your childhood was a roadblock to trusting your parents is what requires your griefwork now. To see if this fits for you, ask yourself if your parents generally:

- Failed to show you the five A's
- Were not attuned to and allowing of your feelings

- Neglected you physically or emotionally
- Abused you physically, emotionally, or sexually
- Had expectations of you that were too low or too high
- Were continually arguing with or abusing each other in your presence
- Used you as a go-between
- Had active addictions

There is a direct connection between unconditional trustworthiness and unconditional love. The yardstick for measuring them is the same. Think now of a family member or friend whom you definitely love and whom you know loves you. This is the person who will stand by you no matter what you do, who will be there for you no matter what you are like, who will remain loyal to you no matter what you become. He is unconditionally trustworthy and unconditionally loving.

Next, think of one whom you do not love quite as much. You may find that the difference in the felt sense of each of them is in your *trust* of them. You fully love the one you fully trust. The one you have some doubts about—that is, the one you do not trust as much—you do not love with the same level of intensity. When someone shows she is trustworthy, she makes the best pitch for our in-depth love.

Show your gratitude to those you deeply love and trust. Their unconditional love is a precious gift, after all.

As a way of not holding anything against those who cannot be trusted so thoroughly, try this: open yourself to compassion for how their judgments, which are a form of suffering, make it hard for them to love as totally as their deeper selves would like to.

A skillful practice is to notice where you are closed and join it to an opening. For example, if you are holding something against someone, try opening to compassion for that person.

This does not excuse his or her shortcoming, only shows you another path to loving-kindness. When that opportunity and success become more important than how people behave, we are standing on a liberating path, so bright in bliss before us.

We can now continue with the practice of loving-kindness. When we love someone, we automatically want that person to be happy and free of suffering. This shows we always knew how to practice loving-kindness. Now all we have to do is apply this kind of loving-kindness to ourselves, to others, and to all beings.

In the traditional Buddhist loving-kindness practice, we wish for happiness, equanimity, and freedom from fear and suffering—first for ourselves, then for those whom we care about, then for those whom we feel neutral about, then for those toward whom we hold negative feelings, then for all beings. This shows how the practice of loving-kindness acknowledges that we are all interdependent. In this modified loving-kindness practice, we aspire for good things first for ourselves, then for the people we especially love, then for those we do not fully trust, and finally for all beings everywhere. Our aspirations are the following: becoming as loving as possible, being happy and fulfilled.

Here is the process, step by step. While doing this practice, it's best to sit in a relaxed but erect and alert posture. You can either close your eyes or keep your eyes open, with your gaze gentle and downward. Say the following phrases to yourself, pausing for a few seconds between each statement:

Phase 1
May I become as loving as possible.
May I be happy.
May I be fulfilled.

Phase 2

May [name of person you love] become as loving as possible.

May [name of person you love] be happy.

May [name of person you love] be fulfilled.

Phase 3

May [name of person you don't fully trust] become as loving as possible.

May [name of person you don't fully trust] be happy.

May [name of person you don't fully trust] be fulfilled.

Loving-kindness also has the meaning of trusting oneself—trusting that we have what it takes to know ourselves thoroughly and completely without feeling hopeless, without turning against ourselves for what we see.

—Pema Chödrön, *Taking the Leap*

3

How Trust Happens
in Relationships

IN OUR EARLIEST HISTORY, we humans huddled together around a campfire, and our trust in one another grew. We were never meant to be alone, not totally, not permanently. We can endure any crisis, navigate our way through any predicament, if only someone stays with us, showing support for us. We do not need someone who will rescue us or take over for us, only someone who will remain by our side, be present, hold a space for what we are going through—not every minute but some of the time. We trust the one who is holding that space for and with us—that is, being present as a fellow human without judging us.

Humans, like all mammals, are geared to live in community, to cooperate and complement one another for survival. Our personal limitations can be compensated for by the assets of others. Our feelings require the mirroring understanding of others. Our courage awakens by encouragement from those we respect. Our fulfillment in love requires a partner who loves us too. This is why abandonment and isolation are so terrifying. This is why having someone who can be trusted to be there for us—be here with us—is essential for our happiness and for a felt sense of being loved.

"Stay with me" is a legitimate and understandable wish, but we have to recognize it as a wish. If the wish comes true with someone, we will cherish the closeness. If we are with someone with whom it never gets past the wish stage, we do not have the makings of a reliable relationship. Evolved people will tire of living with wishes and hopes. In *Peanuts,* more than once, Lucy holds a football so Charlie Brown can kick it, but then she moves it away just before he gets to it. He keeps believing that this time Lucy will not play the same trick on him, with no evidence that she has changed. His wish, not the record, is the basis of his trust, and that does not work. But he does still have the joy of knowing he would not do that to her, and that means a lot too.

An adult upgrades her wish into a request: "Join me in a partnership." This is an explicit offer, not a secret hope or wish. How do we know whether trustworthiness will be forthcoming? We can only go by what the record consistently shows. Trustworthiness has to be put into practice or, as Hamlet said, it "be nothing worth." Likewise, people who are committed to being trustworthy as part of their personal program of integrity are good candidates for trust.

If our deepest desire is to be sought and found by another, and so few people are willing to put energy into that project, we might come to doubt our own value, even our survival. This helps us understand why our most enduring anxiety is about separation, rejection, abandonment, excommunication. These fears can hold such terror for us that we will stay in relationships that no longer work, still clinging to the little that comes our way, still hoping, against evidence to the contrary, that our needs may one day be met. We stay because of the crumbs we occasionally receive, but we also stay because of our fear of the worse isolation that may follow. This is not healthy staying. This is stuckness.

To stay in a healthy sense means to enter the moment fully; to be stuck is to remain frozen, one step removed from our feelings and experience. To stay is to let ourselves go into our own reality so that we can greet what will come next. To be stuck is to refuse to go into it or go on from it. Once again, fear is the culprit that holds us hostage—but it doesn't have to be that way for long. Every practice in this book helps us convert that enemy into an ally. In chapter 5 we will explore in detail our regrettable human penchant to stay stuck in pain.

Although I love you, you will have to leap;
Our dream of safety has to disappear.
—W. H. AUDEN, "LEAP BEFORE YOU LOOK"

Reciprocal Trust

In singles tennis, one player wants to win and wants the other to lose. The other player, likewise, wants to be the one who will win and the other to lose. Each of them pays special attention to the other's defects and plays in such a way as to exploit those liabilities for his own gain. If one player has trouble running fast, the other will be sure to aim the ball so his opponent must dash for it. If one has a poor backhand, the other will be sure to hit the ball so that he needs to use it. The net between the players truly symbolizes their separation.

If, instead, these players become partners in doubles, they notice each other's handicaps, but that shows them how to cooperate and cover for each other. Now the goal is for both to

win rather than only one to win. In a relationship, both partners are meant to play together as just such a team. Trust happens when we notice we are with a partner who is committed
to playing with us for our mutual victory over the obstacles that
can wreck our bond. Now the net symbolizes being together.
We play with reciprocal attentiveness, and each of us backs the
other up. It will take letting go of self-centeredness in favor of
sharing authentic love to play like that.

Trust has to be reciprocal for relationships to work. This
means each partner can *trust* the other and each partner is *trustworthy* toward the other. Trust and trustworthiness are not
only sources of safety and security. They make an intimate relationship possible, increase love, and enrich the bond. In all
these ways, trust and trustworthiness fulfill our growth needs.

In the romance phase of a relationship, we trust the other
implicitly and unconditionally. We feel sure of the stability of
the love we are receiving. This is also why we fall the hardest if
perfidy happens during that stage of a relationship. Wise adults
begin relationships not with the romance phase but with an
investigation phase. We check out the other, looking to see if
he or she is trustworthy, has the ability to give the five A's, and
possesses the qualities that are important to us. Only when we
are secure in the knowledge that the other is trustworthy do we
open ourselves to letting love happen. This means that even
chemistry cannot be trusted as a criterion. Only ongoing obser-
vation works, and even that can prove to be inaccurate, but at
least we tried our best at being Sherlock Holmes.

Romantic fascination toward someone—chemistry—is exciting in two ways. Our needy ego is excited by the possibility
of finding fulfillment at last. But our healthy ego is excited too
because we have located just the person who will show us
where our work is, our unfinished conflicts from childhood or

past relationships. Thus, some enchanted evening, we find both our soul mate and our soul's work. The needy ego may blame his partner later. The healthy ego will thank her.

If we struggle with low self-esteem and a partner is proved trustworthy, we might say, "She makes me feel so good that I forget my uphill battle with self-worth. I am dependent on her now to help me feel good about myself, and she dare not go off duty because I can't provide that for myself." This is not the foundation of a healthy relationship. We do not require our partner to give us more than about 25 percent of our total need for the five A's (attention, acceptance, appreciation, affection, and allowing). No single person should be expected to fulfill all or even most of our emotional needs.

Once we are independent, we align ourselves to those who are consistently trustworthy. Adult trust is based on the proven trustworthiness of the other. Our adult trust grows best in an atmosphere of continuity and consistency. Yet we have no control over that happening. This is why trust sails in a fragile bark. We can trust in trustworthiness only when it is happening and cease trusting when it ends. Nonetheless, it is perfectly reasonable for us to rely on others to keep agreements and not to betray us.

Thus, trust takes hold in a relationship when someone shows himself to be reliable. It ends when it turns out that he is not. It begins again if he changes for the better. It ends if he changes for the worse. Yearning for someone to trust absolutely is how we keep ourselves feeling unhappy. We are forgetting the first teaching of Buddhism, that all is ultimately unreliable, impermanent, and therefore unsatisfactory, and that we suffer when we cling to something with the illusory belief that such is not so. And it also happens that some people have shown themselves to be unconditionally and enduringly trustworthy toward us. Then we have something lasting to cherish and be thankful for. Nevertheless, we balance that realization with the wisdom of impermanence generally.

In any case, we don't get to decide how long others' feelings for us will endure or how strong they will be. An adult has learned to honor the shelf life of a feeling and the life span of trust. Wisdom in relationships can take the form of aligning or resigning ourselves to how far the other can go, how close she can allow herself to be to us, how much of a commitment she can make to a relationship with us. Our goal is to open a space and in that space to say yes to what is and to what can be, moving *toward* when that is appropriate, moving *on* when that is what fits best.

Adults know that trust cannot be based on expectations or projections. Nor can others be presumed trustworthy because we believe we are entitled to their loyalty or have merited it. The ego has to bow in total surrender to the ruthless record of real instances of trustworthiness or betrayal. When we have an adult outlook, this does not lead us to turn on those who do not come through. Instead, we say "Ouch" aloud to them, grieve our loss, and move on without trying to get back at them. This aligns with the Dalai Lama's instruction to be angry at the deed but not to harm the doer.

We investigate others; we keep a watch on ourselves. Since trust takes time to develop, it is important for us to protect our boundaries in new relationships. We do this when we let our disclosure of our deeper selves happen only in increments. We have to be careful not to overexpose, not to self-disclose too soon.

Over the course of our lives, we eventually become sophisticated about what the world and others are like. We become centered so that we are neither gullible nor cynical. We become compassionate because we realize that it is sometimes hard for any of us humans to be trustworthy. So instead of despairing or retaliating in return, we remain loyal to two spiritual practices: loving-kindness and an unconditional yes to what is. Loving-kindness directs our focus to building our own trustworthiness and aspiring for it in others. Our companion practice of the unconditional yes to what is directs us to be thankful for trustworthiness from others when it comes our way and be open to disappointment sometimes too.

If we are the ones who act in an untrustworthy way, we may inappropriately insist that our partner trust us even though we have often deceived her. We see the contradiction between the demand that we be respected and our bad record. Our practice is to make amends and commit ourselves to change. Then a shift occurs, and we stop demanding that our partner trust us but rather let the record of our new behavior show her the difference in us. Patience has replaced demand. Willingness to make amends and to amend our life has replaced the ego's belief that there is no need for amends. This is an altogether healthy option, letting trust of us arise in others, or not, as we let go of manipulating them, while acting in full integrity no matter what the outcome. We can usually *feel* the rightness of that path. A sociopath, someone with no guilt or loyalty, scorns that feeling as sentimental or as nonapplicable.

Trusting, in the realm of relationship, leads to opening ourselves to another, revealing ourselves to another, relying on the other to come through for us. This means taking a risk, because all humans have the capacity to fail or deceive us. Yet it is a risk worth taking if the record shows that so far the other has been dependable, that the trust is reciprocal. We can also take the risk of trusting in the absence of any data or evidence, as long as we are willing to accept the consequences. These words from *Hamlet* describe the vulnerability in that risk:

> Exposing what is mortal and unsure
> To all that fortune, death, and danger
> dare. . . .

Surrender in a Committed Relationship

As long as our own serenity, safety, and security are based on someone's fidelity to us, we remain in that person's power. The yes of surrender to the limits in our relationship leads to serenity, the safety and security that happen from within us. Such surrender is our proof to ourselves that we really can trust ourselves. We begin to redirect our trust, an empowering venture.

Trusting ourselves means letting go of control and saying yes to the possibility of disloyalty and disillusionment. "I have to be in control" means giving up hope in resources beyond our own ego. The five A's toward others, with loving-kindness as our spiritual practice, help free us from needing to be in control.

We all encounter selfish and disloyal people in the course of life, and we suffer as a result. As we grow in spiritual consciousness, we see their suffering too. Selfishness and disloyalty are forms of constriction that oppose a person's natural inclination toward openness, thus causing stress, suffering. We can bring both ourselves and them into our loving-kindness practice. Sooner or later, we can come to see the shadow side of humanity, not as a reason for pessimism but as an opportunity for practicing compassion.

Surrender to another happens when we can truly trust her. Surrender to reality happens when we accept what she wants to be for us. Then what we see as her deficits and excesses become interesting to us; we see them with curiosity but not with desolation or terror. We can decide where to go from there and how to bargain for what we need.

The partner who surrenders to the reality of who the other is notices the shape a relationship is taking but does not try to control its direction. Here is what aligning to the reality of the other may sound like to a man who is dating: "I enjoy her company, and I notice she enjoys mine. At the same time, she has many male friends with whom she shares her feelings and ideas at what seems like quite an intimate level. I want to honor that support system. I trust that her friendships are all as platonic as she says, yet doubts arise sometimes. I don't want to jump to conclusions. I don't want to demand that I be the one and only. But I do want to become special and primary if she is open to that. I can let go of that wish if it can't match reality, to which I owe my main loyalty. I will open a dialogue with her about all this, state my concerns, and present my wish. I won't do this all at once but time it all in accord with what seems right for both of us." This is the healthy alternative to "I can't trust any woman who has this many male friends."

In the example above, the surrender is to the reality of what the relationship is about. The more challenging surrender is to a person, to a commitment to a relationship of trust. It is said that we men have problems surrendering to someone because it feels as if we are giving up our freedom, something we may cling to as our most prized possession. This is why we so often feel a fear of closeness and commitment, actually a fear of trusting how we will feel in the midst of those experiences. We imagine we will be suffocated, trapped, engulfed if closeness happens; we will be unable to maintain our personal identity, something we associate with being separate. We may certainly seek some form of connection but with no strings attached.

It may take a partner a long time to convince us that it is safe to love her unreservedly. She will have to be willing to allow a long series of open-ended experiences, ones in which the door is continually visible and open in case we need to make a fast getaway. It may be hard for us to find someone with that kind of patience, and would we respect someone willing to be that self-sacrificing with no promise of return?

A woman might offer this response to the male fear of commitment: "I am glad to notice that I no longer need to caretake men. If they want help with their difficulties in surrendering to a relationship, I suggest professional therapy. Men who want a relationship with me but see it as giving up their freedom should keep it."

Ironically, we men who fear losing our freedom often have no difficulty surrendering to an addiction (the word *addiction* is based on the Latin for "surrender"). Our addiction certainly is a form of "giving up our freedom," but that does not stop us. Our "fear of commitment" vanishes when it comes to giving ourselves over to what has come to seem so necessary for us—for example, alcohol, drugs, sex, gambling. This reveals to us men that we do not as much fear surrender as fear trusting who we will become in full-on intimacy with someone real. This is an identity anxiety; we can't be separate anymore. *How can we men move toward allowing seasons of change as the caterpillar does?*

The alcoholic male knows from solid experience how to avoid being found out. He knows that a drink will relieve him of any anxiety when he is experiencing intense feeling or at the edge of being recognized for precisely what he is. He knows that his emptiness will be immediately and effectively compensated for by the ingestion of a drug, and he will then feel adequate, even triumphant. His fear of being caught in something bigger than himself, something that will crash through his autonomy, is quelled.

Thus, regarding relationship, we may have a fear of surrender that holds us back. Yet we can wholeheartedly surrender in other areas, no matter what the hazards. The more reflective we become about ourselves, the more suspicious we will be of ourselves. The twelve-step programs offer the "gentle patience" that helps to free us from our addictions. But, of course, that will take surrender of ego, surrender of addiction, and surrender to the program that leads to the risk of trusting a power beyond ourselves.

Addiction is a displacement of our need for affirmation or affiliation onto alcohol or sex or any other object of addiction. Since we live in such a competitive world, people are not usually looking for ways to make us feel good about ourselves. In fact, some may want to kick us in the shins so we won't succeed. The continuing scandals involving addicted sports and political idols show us that even the highly successful seek an affirmation that no amount of success in those areas seems to fulfill. The person, place, or thing we become addicted to is like our old teddy bear, a transitional object when the life-sustaining comforts of Mom are not accessible. We were learning to substitute way back then, and now keep doing it, except this time not always to our advantage, though our addictions may seem fuzzy-feeling nonetheless.

The twelve-step programs have at their heart the counsel to surrender, to tell our story without cushioning it, to trust that acknowledging powerlessness is the path to true power, to the strength to manage one's life. This happens especially since the program offers affirmation and affiliation, life-sustaining comforts that are always accessible. What a useful and supportive path to trusting others and finally to trusting ourselves. *Is this what we have feared all along?*

We need not be addicts to have this growth-enhancing experience. We can find it in a healthy relationship with someone who loves us and also offers affirmation, affiliation, and life-sustaining comforts. In addition, we can find it without an intimate relationship. It resides in meaningful friendships and in associations with others who share our passions. All these enterprises with others help us toward adulthood because their affirmative comforts teach us to self-soothe. Then we can even be alone happily too. That completes the human cycle from our needs to others' resources to self-fulfillment.

To Whom Shall We Go?

Most mammals, when they are in danger, go somewhere for safety—for example, a rabbit runs into a hole. However, primates run to someone. Humans not only go to some other human but may also go to Someone transcendent for support. However, all mammals soon learn to defend themselves in some way while staying within the safety of their group. This, as we have just seen, reflects our human development from safety and security found in others to safety and security in ourselves while still remaining in relationship to our support system, the equivalent in the primate world of the troupe or band.

The one to whom we can go when we are in distress is the one we trust. We trust the person who has not let us down in the past and who, we believe, will not do so now. We trust because we feel a secure and enduring connection. It is in the arms of someone that we can most often calm ourselves and reconstitute after a disruption of or threat to our serenity. A healthy relationship is one in which each partner can securely go to the other when that need arises. As we get into the roller coaster for the first time, we feel safe if someone who is unafraid is joining us. Then we can feel our fear in the presence of someone who is not afraid but accompanies us in our fear. Somehow that works to give us courage.

Our primary object of trust will always be the person who fulfills our primary needs. Emotionally speaking, our primary needs, in childhood and throughout life, are the five A's. Trust happens in just such an atmosphere. We can rely on the one who loves us to pay *attention* to us, to *accept* us as we are, to *appreciate* and value us, to show us *affection* in appropriate ways, and to *allow* us to live freely without attempting to control us. An adult with self-confidence will trust someone only when those five A's are visible daily. Now we see what is really meant by reliance on reliability.

A trustworthy partner, the one we can go to, is one who will stay with us through a conflict: "I know you love me and will stay with me through this crisis we are having. Your focus will be on working through our conflict, not on making sure you win." Mutual trust means: "I can be in conflict with you but with no sense of threat. You will not punish me and I will not punish you. I will still be here when the smoke clears and so will you." Staying power is a crucial clue to someone's trustworthiness.

A healthy relationship is one in which staying consists of a continual addressing, processing, resolving, and integrating of struggles. When that program is not in place for both parties, we have no basis for trusting that a relationship can work. There is no commitment when denial and avoidance take the place of addressing. We have no bond when refusal to show feeling or explore issues cancels our chances at processing our concerns. There is no contentment when a conflict in a relationship is not resolved but smolders instead. Then our experience cannot be integrated into our lives as an opportunity to grow.

Our past is often littered with misattunements, prohibitions against full emergence, slaps for daring to go further than allowed. This is the old business we become able to clear up when we address our present conflicts. We might despair that such a venture can ever happen in the context of our present relationship. We might despair of ever being seen or heard. We give up on trying to work things out before we have really tried. Then we shut down the palace of possibility and, as John Donne lamented, "A great prince in prison lies."

Our history however, does not *have* to interfere with our initiatives. We can take our chances and show a little more of who we are anyway. This time we may find attunement. This time we may not need it quite so much. If we are prohibited in some way, we can try once more. Such risking is the trust that frees us. The following practice helps us toward that freedom.

Exploring Our Style of Trusting

We may notice ourselves going through phases in seeking someone to trust in a relationship. The stages are reminiscent of what British psychiatrist John Bowlby discovered in his work with displaced and orphaned children. We reach out to others we imagine we can trust; we are angry at them if they prove untrustworthy; we fall into despair about being able to trust them, or sometimes anyone, thereafter.

The shift from reaching out to becoming angry reflects our frustration that our most basic, innate needs are not being honored. We feel impotent and enraged because we believe we deserve to have others respond to us. The second shift, from rage to despair about trusting others at all, is more subtle. We may not notice it for years. We may call it wise reserve, independence, caution, or even spiritual detachment. But, in reality, it is the loss of hope in other humans, no longer trusting contactfulness. This chart may help us see how the three phases play out:

Reaching Out	*Becoming Enraged*	*Falling into Despair*
We reach out to make contact.	We become angry that the other is not responsive to us or has betrayed or abandoned us.	We give up believing that trust can be found in this or in any relationship.
We make sure to look our best and be on our best behavior so we can impress someone.	We may retaliate.	We avoid intimacy altogether.

We are animated by joy and enthusiasm.	We are driven by disappointment and failed entitlement.	We are caught in an attitude of "sour grapes" and un-willingness to take another chance.

When the Five A's Meet the Ego

Each of the five A's exists in contrast to an egotistic style that can lead us to mistrust others:

The Intimate Way	*The Neurotic Ego's Way*
Attention	Self-absorption
Acceptance	Judgment and criticism
Appreciation	Indifference or blame
Affection	Distancing
Allowing	Controlling

The practice of the five A's is a path out of grandiose narcissism into the possibility of relatedness:

Paying attention to a partner frees a person from self-absorption.

Acceptance of the other frees a partner from judgment of the other.

Appreciation is a loving alternative to indifference and resentment.

Showing affection without always demanding that it lead to sex facilitates a rich and deep closeness.

Letting go of control makes it possible to honor the freedom of the other, the real meaning of allowing.

In an insecure attachment to someone, our nervous system is always on the lookout for nonattunement, a deficiency of the five A's. Those disruptions of the smooth continuity of intimacy have to be repaired if a relationship is to succeed. Delay leads to an erosion of trust. This is why addressing relationship problems is so necessary in the building of trust. A commitment to a continual mending of failures by making amends for them is what makes trustworthiness real.

The way we choose to avoid our personal pain is always the same as the way we avoid confronting our mutual problems. For instance, an affair helps us avoid the dissatisfaction we feel in our relationship. It can be used to avoid the uphill work of healing it by addressing, processing, and resolving the real issues in the primary relationship. That program will take a willingness to let go of ego entitlement and will require us to declare our pain. It will take a combination of humility and assertiveness. That will be hard to muster if we have not been practicing it all along. Here is where we see clearly why practices for letting go of ego are so important in the toolbox of successful intimacy.

Now we are ready to ask, How can we know when it is wise to trust a partner? The answer will encapsulate what we have learned in this chapter so far. It is wise to trust when we see at least these six factors consistently present in the relationship:

1. Sincere work on letting go of ego for the success of the relationship.
2. A continual giving of the five A's, shown by attunement to our feelings.
3. The abiding sense that the relationship offers a secure base from which each partner can explore and a safe haven to which each can return.
4. A series of kept agreements.
5. Mutuality in decision making.
6. A willingness to work problems out with each other by addressing, processing, resolving them together. This

includes a willingness to declare our pain about what is missing in the relationship and our appreciation of what is fulfilling.

These six also serve as the definition of long-term commitment. Trust then can be defined as what happens in us in response to evidence that a commitment has been made to us. Otherwise, we live on guard and our ego has to grow proportionally as our protector, albeit always afraid underneath.

An abused child will abuse other children, often in the same way and for the same reasons that he was abused. This happens in the realm of trust too. People with a long history of betrayals of trust tend not be trustworthy. They may be abusive or controlling instead.

Now we understand what can happen when the ego meets the five A's. The ego gets a chance to downgrade its overdrawn authority along with its fear and stress in favor of the love that the five A's represent and produce.

Each of the five A's given by us to a partner or by her to us leads to a boost in self-esteem. Thus, attention leads to a sense of being cared about and valued. Acceptance leads to the possibility of changing for the better. Appreciation leads to a sense of being approved, admired, and understood. Affection gives us a positive feeling toward our body. Allowing confirms us in our right to our choices. Self-esteem is defined as those five results of the five A's: being valued; making useful changes; being approved, admired, and understood; being pleased about our body; and having the space to make the choices that reflect who we are.

Practices for Auditing Our Relationship

This chart helps us see the difference between trust and trustworthiness and prepares us for the practices below:

Trust	Trustworthiness
Having confidence in someone else's trustworthiness	*Being oneself deserving of trust*
Conditional	Unconditional
Reliant	Reliable
A belief	A personal quality
Gained by experience	Gained by practice
Based on others' behavior	Based on personal standards
Requires continual discernment of others' motives and actions	Is a conscientious commitment that requires no response in kind
Can be violated by others	Cannot be influenced by what others do
Can be misplaced because of an illusory projection on our part or reliance on a false promise on the part of someone else	Is given to others with sincerity and as part of personal integrity
May be temporary	Is permanent
Is a capacity originating in early life within a psychologically healthy environment	Is a virtue that begins and grows with spiritual consciousness
Seeks safety and security in others	Has found safety and security in oneself

HOW TO KNOW IF SOMEONE CAN BE TRUSTED

Use this expanded checklist to audit your relationship with regard to your partner toward you and you toward him or her.

Show this list and your responses to it to your partner. Ask him or her to use the same list regarding you. If you or your partner are not truly described by this list of positive qualities, discuss what action you can take to change things for the better.

MY PARTNER

☐ Shows integrity and lives in accord with standards of fairness and honesty in *all* his or her dealings. (There is a connection between integrity and trust in the *Webster's Dictionary* definition: "Trust is the assured reliance on another's integrity.")

☐ May operate on the basis of self-interest but never at my expense or the expense of others.

☐ Will not retaliate, use the silent treatment, resort to violence, or hold a grudge.

☐ Predictably shows me the five A's.

☐ Supports me when I need him or her.

☐ Keeps agreements.

☐ Remains faithful.

☐ Does not lie or have a secret life.

☐ Genuinely cares about me.

☐ Stands by me and up for me.

☐ Is what he or she appears to be; wants to appear just as he or she is, no matter if at times that is unflattering.

☐ Respects my boundaries—for instance, when I say no, he will back off. Tries to work things out by addressing, processing, and resolving issues as they arise. This means that his or her presence in my life has become reliable. In the face of difficulties and conflicts, it is not

"Get me outta here," as the Cowardly Lion would say, but "I still will stay with thee," as Romeo would.

☐ Does not jump to finding a solution when I tell him or her of a problem in my life but rather looks for ways to deepen his or her feelings about the problem and carefully inquire into what I really need in that moment.

☐ Can listen without judgment (without a fixed or moralistic belief). I do not find myself saying or thinking, "He/she doesn't hear me." I notice that my partner is listening attentively to my words, my feelings, and my body language too. The ability to hear someone is really about trust, not simply about communication. A trust issue always lurks beneath a communication difficulty.

☐ Does not give up on me or on anyone. My partner continues to believe in the inherent goodness and potential for enlightenment in everyone and believes that problems between himself or herself and others are workable. When others refuse that option and demand that my partner stay away, however, he or she gets the message and pulls back.

☐ Is more committed to being honest about his or her mistakes and apologizing when necessary than in defending his or her ego. A partner who can't admit he was wrong but instead loudly insists he was justified in his unkind behavior is not a good candidate for intimacy. Imagine that same kind of ego in a doctor—or a president. (I recall an interview in which Henry Kissinger said that Richard Nixon did not end the war in Vietnam early on in his terms because "he did not want to be remembered as the president who lost a war." Imagine having a son in the army with that attitude in the White House.)

We can take both trustworthiness and untrustworthiness as information about whether a relationship can go on but never as an incentive to hurt back if we are betrayed or to stay put if we are hurt.

We can also do an audit of our sex life:

☐ How interested am I in being sexual with you?

☐ How delighted am I by seeing you, being with you, or thinking about you?

☐ How is our sexuality contributing to our intimacy?

☐ Can we be intimate without having to be sexual every time?

We share these questions and our answers with our partner and ask for her answers.

The five A's are how we show that we have taken an *interest* in a partner rather than simply clinging to one because of how needy we are. Healthy people have noticed *that* interest as a more sincere form of connection than sexual excitement or clinging. Sincere interest in the other makes the five A's part of every sexual and intimate experience. Is that happening?

An audit can be successful only when both partners can be fully adult in how they handle it. A good audit has to be followed by recommendations for improvement, not blame or retaliation. This is the kind of sincerity, defenselessness, and honesty most people would not dare allow or approach. But with psychological work and a commitment to spiritual practice of some kind, we can. *Do my partner and I respond to each other with honesty and openness rather than defensiveness?*

A competent auditor remains somewhat suspicious until convinced otherwise. Here is an example of how psychological auditing might take shape. We question ourselves about the kind of trustworthiness we are demanding. For instance, this statement sounds acceptable: "I want a deeper commitment from him." Yet if we audit our desire, we might find three suspicious implications. First, it seems to include this childlike wish: "I want to be sure he will never disappoint me." This cannot be an adult expectation, since it contradicts the givens of existence. As long as we are looking for total safety, we are not honoring life as it is. As long as we are trying to line up a relationship that assures us of full protection against any form of disenchantment, we are still afraid of being adults.

Second, the statement subtly includes trying to control the other's behavior. The rugged individualist needs to be in full control at all times, so relating in a trusting way is hard for him. He thinks being in control makes him secure, but that only makes him insecure about how to stay in control. Trying to be in control is another form of hanging on to what becomes a noose.

Third, the original statement is suspicious spiritually, since it seeks to make a human being one's higher power, a transcendently reliable source beyond ego.

HOW COMMUNICATION BECOMES TRUSTWORTHY

A trustworthy person is committed to being assertive but not aggressive. Assertiveness is motivated by self-esteem and respect for others. Aggression is motivated by the need for ego satisfaction. We can ask ourselves which style is ours and whether we want to upgrade from aggression to assertiveness if necessary. Most of us are afraid of being assertive at all and remain passive. A commitment to sincere assertiveness frees us from the fear of being ourselves. That makes us open to forming intimate relationships. So practicing healthy assertiveness is a way of being capable of real love. Do we dare?

Reflect on the following chart to assess whether your style is more assertive or aggressive.

Assertive	*Aggressive*
Based on willingness to show others our needs and feelings	*Based on fear that we will not be in control*
We have real *power* and are not threatened if others have power too: we seek power for and with others.	We keep trying to gain *control* and to stay in a one-up position: we seek power over others.
Our distress leads us to addressing, processing, resolving it.	Our distress leads automatically to aggression so we can regain control.
We present our agenda and needs clearly.	We force our agenda on others directly or indirectly.
We ask for what we want, and always with courtesy.	We demand what we want and/or tell the other what to do.
We can take no for an answer, and we back off.	We keep pushing until the other gives in: "Twist his arm until he knuckles under!"
We use "I" statements.	We use "you" statements.
We respect the boundaries of others.	We disregard the boundaries of others.
We honestly say yes, no, or maybe and show our preferences and boundaries.	We say what seems to be the best strategy to manipulate others.

We ask others to be clear about their needs, and we are willing to listen to them even if what they say is not to our liking.

We are so caught up in our own wishes that we do not listen to others or care about their ideas or needs.

We show our feelings respectfully so as to let others know where we are coming from.

We show our feelings dramatically in order to intimidate, threaten, attack, or bully.

We show others respect at all times, treating them as peers.

We put others down, treating them as objects.

We model the behavior we want to evoke.

We behave toward others in ways that we would not tolerate from them toward us.

We ask that others take responsibility for their behavior.

We blame or shame others for their behavior.

We *want* to get ahead but look for ways to let others feel empowered too.

We *have* to win, even if it means hurting or humiliating others.

We try to work things out so that all can benefit.

We are focused only on getting our own way.

We realize that what happens may not match what we want, but we are committed to negotiating creative alternatives that can meet more of everyone's needs.

We are compulsive about having everything work out exactly as we *have* to have it, irrespective of others' needs.

We are nonviolent in word and behavior.

We are abusive, sarcastic, or insulting.

We stand up for our reasonable rights.

We insist on special privileges.

Assertive (contd.)	*Aggressive (contd.)*
We let others know the impact of their behavior on us, saying "Ouch!" and "Don't!" when it is negative and "Thanks!" when it is positive.	We react to the impact of others' behavior on us with criticism or contempt if it is negative and not necessarily with appreciation if it is positive.
We ask for amends but do not retaliate if they are not forthcoming.	We seek to get back at those who dare to disappoint our expectations.
We act in our own best interest without trespassing on the rights of others: we believe that rights bring responsibilities, and we are willing to act accordingly.	We act in our own best interests no matter who gets hurt in the process: our belief is that we have entitlements without corresponding responsibilities.
We live by and act on a coopera-tive model.	We live by and act on a dominator model.
These are forms of conscious creative communication that deepen relationships.	*These are habit-driven declarations that sabotage healthy communication.*

This chart presents the two extreme ends of a spectrum of behavior. Between these two extremes, we can imagine columns that include passivity and other communication options, too numerous to list.

If you found yourself mostly on the aggressive side of this chart, choose one or two items on the list and for one week make a conscious effort to adopt the assertive style instead.

4

How We Miss Trust

IN THE 1946 FILM *Deception,* Christine Radcliffe, played by Bette Davis, has been involved with a man who has financed an affluent lifestyle for her. She breaks off the relationship to marry the man she really loves, who has just returned from Europe, where she knew him years ago. However, she does not reveal to him that she had been involved with someone else. The husband soon becomes suspicious, especially after meeting the former lover. But Christine insists that he had always been and remains only a friend. The husband realizes he cannot fully trust his wife's words. Finally, her former lover threatens to expose her, and Christine kills him to protect her secret. In the movie's final scene, she does a surprising thing. She confesses the murder to her husband and admits that the man she killed was indeed her lover. Just before leaving for the police station to give herself up, she declares to her husband that she suddenly feels "closer" to him than she ever has before. The newfound closeness was the result of her finally being truthful, finally becoming trustworthy. I saw a look of joy, contentment, and relief on her face (as only Bette Davis could show).

Watching this film recently, I asked myself, "I wonder if we lie to each other and hide *because we fear that deeper level of closeness?*" Then lying is a way of managing our fear of intimacy. The cover-up helps us avoid what feels so threatening. We imagine, as Christine did, that we are keeping our secrets because we want to maintain and protect our privacy or avoid embarrassment, but that may be a rationalization. Our real goal may be to stave off genuine, face-to-face, heart-to-heart closeness. How ironic that we are avoiding exactly what will make us truly happy, truly liberated, truly contented—the very gifts that relationships are meant to offer.

Our secrets are, tragically, our way of preventing the full fruition of trust in us by another and of trustworthiness in ourselves. In the film, the wife could not be trustworthy until it was time to separate. Are there some of us who cannot allow a relationship of trust if we know we will be together the next day and every day thereafter?

The story in the film also shows how fear and mistrust are related. The Bette Davis character, in effect, was saying to her husband, "I am afraid to reveal myself to you because you might use it against me or leave me because of it." This is mistrust, not fear. She doesn't really trust his love to be unconditional. Here is another example of how we might feel fear when we actually have a trust issue.

Fear of trusting can also be based on an intelligent assessment of someone's lack of trustworthiness, as was felt by the husband in the film. Such hesitancy about trusting specific people and circumstances may be an accurate intuition on our part. Our next step is to check out our intuitive sense to see if it matches reality. We can, of course, override the intuition—and the experience—in moments of passion or addiction.

Trusting Can Wake Old Ghosts

Trusting may evoke unconscious fears, hand-me-downs from the past when we had trusted someone but then were deceived. These deceits and betrayals conditioned us to associate our trusting with being hurt by others. *Conscious trusting in the present brings up unconscious associations from the past, and they feel real now.* This is such an important piece of psychological information to have, especially when we first love someone. We wonder why we feel anxious. It could be a simple case of stimulus and response. The trusting is the stimulus that triggers the memory of how it led to pain in the past. A new experience evokes an old pattern. Past experiences of violated trust leave post-traumatic scars. In the present, what hampers us is not our experience of trust itself but our freeze reaction to it. Time stands still, and the past interrupts and usurps the present.

Trauma therapy shows how our body can be a resource in dealing with our stress reaction stemming from abuse in early life. This happens not by minimizing the facts but by redesigning our relationship to them. We cannot rewrite our story, but we can rewire our brain. This happens when our memories remain intact but without the emotional charge that can cause ongoing damage to our capacity to trust. Such damage shows up in adult relationships as fears of closeness or commitment and especially as fear of trusting. Therapy aimed at working through trauma can integrate our narrative so that we are no longer driven by these fears. In addition, once our abuse story is held with the five A's, it can be demoted from a disabling fear to a nearly flatline fact—what Emily Dickinson calls "almost peace." Our belief about ourselves then changes from victim to victor-with-shrapnel, not so bad a title, given our story.

We are so fragile that even the most ordinary early rejection and deception can become traumatic and freeze our lively trust in ourselves. With no emotional resources, the only way to deal with our pain is to store it in the unconscious. Then, as soon as we trust someone, a conditioned response arises. We begin to feel fear or even suspicion, rooted in actual past experience, but perhaps now having no foundation in reality. We imagine our doubt to be an intuition about danger, but it is actually the past being replayed in the present. We have opened the file called "Trust in Others," and in it are archives of ache. That file remains open until we have a long history of tried-and-true trustworthiness from someone.

This is especially dicey because every new relationship, no matter how promising, presents derivatives, reminders, and remainders of our past. Our unconscious motivation is always to complete the past and to heal it by finding that trustworthy someone. Our conscious mind seeks a sequel (our story moving forward), but our unconscious finds a remake, a retelling of the story with new characters, who are hired on to resolve business, not theirs but ours. This is transference of the past onto the present.

When we realized that our childhood home was dysfunctional and we found a healthy way to separate from it, we are less likely to be affected by it in the present. However, the more enmeshed we were in our family's emotional life, the more the past hangs on deleteriously in us. For instance, in her childhood, Concetta's parents were caught up in drama and addiction. She believed she had to take care of them, and they, inappropriately, relied on her to do so. Concetta may have felt frustration or guilt because she failed to fix them.

Because of her childhood conditioning, there is a connection in Concetta's mind between being there for others and being disappointed by others, and now she fears commitment. Even if she has broken the old bond to her parents and no longer lets their story manipulate her, the past is still so strongly imprinted in Concetta that it obstructs her capacity to trust another adult. Though her rational mind tells her she has a good partner, she still has doubts. This may feel to her like a reasonable suspicion about his trustworthiness, but it is really about her own fear of commitment to anyone. How ironic that Concetta's trustworthiness toward her parents makes her unable to receive trustworthiness now.

In addition, since Concetta's father and mother were continually unfaithful to each other, Concetta despairs that a relationship can work at all. This too hangs on in her as a gnawing uneasiness. The memory stored in every cell of her body keeps waving its red flag. Only grieving her past and releasing it can ready Concetta for a successful adult relationship.

This is an example of how a problem in a relationship is often actually a personal problem requiring personal work. This work will help Concetta break the old tie of misplaced loyalty. Then a new tie can form, and, perhaps for the first time, she can feel held.

Transference is a psychological term for this triggering of childhood issues in an adult relationship. We transfer our feelings toward a person from the past onto someone in the present. Thus, a partner may raise his voice in anger at us, and this immediately evokes the same disempowering fear that we felt in childhood when our father shouted at us and became violent. This is not necessarily a relationship problem but our own issue, since a raised voice is a normal part of anger.

We may notice ourselves going through three phases as we work on our transference: At first we feel overwhelmed, and the stress or emotional charge is long-lasting. As we address and work through our pain from the past, we enter phase two: the same intense reaction but with a shorter shelf life. We know we are resolving things when in phase three there is considerably less or no intensity and no lasting result. Now we are stabilizing ourselves almost immediately because the power of the original childhood events has lost its punch. We are more secure in ourselves because we have become resilient in our relationships.

We may place our trust in someone because of transference. This happens when someone evokes the sense of safety and security that we felt in the past. When that old familiar and still-needed sense of familial comfort arises, we may interpret that as a sign that we have found the right person for us. It may even feel like chemistry between us. Until we tease out the connection to the past and experience this person as herself, we do not know whether she is the candidate for us. This is how our attachment, based on the warm feeling of safety and security, can hurl us into an illusion, as Buddhist teaching reminds us.

Intimate relationships bring up transferences more powerfully than friendships do. This is why friendships often work so much more easily than intimate relationships. They do not activate our early-life issues the way a primary relationship does. So they often remain relatively uncomplicated, mostly stress-free, unless more than friendship is afoot—namely, transference. At the same time, we may notice that the friends we most enjoy being with are the ones who create an atmosphere of cozy safety and security, and we appreciate the comfort in that.

One way to dodge having to address our early-life issues is to maintain only shallow or short-term relationships with partners who do not call us on our behavior. We may seek only sex and light companionship from our relationships. As soon as we are challenged to face the conflicted areas from our past, we abandon the relationship. But at some point, we realize we do not have to run. A relationship has special value to us precisely because it offers us unique access to our early conflicts.

Here's an example of how the past can complicate our present: When meeting someone new, we may feel nervous and insecure: "Will she like me? Will I measure up to what she wants?" But our anxiety may not be related only to such conscious and obvious self-doubts. On the unconscious level, we are fearing that this meeting or relationship may become a replay of betrayals or disappointments from people who hurt us in our past, either during childhood or as recently as last year. Our self-protective mechanism is overactivated because of past burns that now make us twice shy. That may be the major part of our fear.

It's essential to discover the trust issue that underlies our fear in relationships. When we focus on our fears, we put the accent on the external threat from a person, place, or thing—real or imagined. For example, someone with a fear of intimacy may candidly say, "I am uncomfortable with your brand of closeness. It comes across as clinging, and that scares me. So let's work out a way of being together that we both can live with." Awareness of the fear has led to the possibility of addressing, processing, resolving it in an interpersonal forum.

When we notice that we cannot trust our own reactions, we're seeing that we still do not trust *ourselves*. Now the accent is on the internal concern; we are taking responsibility for what is happening inside us. Then we might sound like this: "I don't trust myself to handle closeness from women because I believe that I either won't be able to tolerate my own feelings when they get close or won't be able to protect my boundaries when they approach me." Now the issue is about ourselves, and we have more personal rather than relationship work to do. We are fearing the other in the first instance; we are doubting our own ability with anyone in the second instance.

A specifically focused fear—that is, a fear about a particular person who seems to be untrustworthy—may be realistic and accurate, a form of discrimination. A fear of trusting anyone at all is not necessary or realistic. No matter how untrustworthy someone was toward us, there are truly trustworthy people in the world nonetheless. Our distrust is bias, not knowledge.

The overall fear of trusting can also indicate that our original foundation in trust was unsuccessfully installed or so misaligned that our ability to trust was canceled altogether. Such a fear of trusting ever again points to work we can do on ourselves. We can examine our past to see how and where trust did or did not happen. When we grieve our past, it no longer has to determine how we act or feel in relationships now. There is always hope that we can learn to trust again.

Most intimacy fears are about the risk of trusting. Our fear of commitment may take the form of unilaterally bowing out of relationships once intimacy begins to happen. We then are trusting that our fear is wiser than our love. We can break the cycle by bringing up our fears as soon as we feel them. Then they sit between us and our partner—like the net in tennis doubles—rather than in our own heads.

When we report our fears to each other, we can accurately assess them. When we hear ourselves finally saying it all out loud, we receive new information about ourselves. When we hear our partner's reply, we have information about her. The honesty leads to a mutual ability to repair our relationship so love can flourish.

In fact, we automatically become more courageous when we have someone to love. For instance, in the film *The Wizard of Oz,* when the time comes to save Dorothy from the castle of the wicked witch, Cowardly Lion wants to bow out because of his fear. He becomes willing when two things become clear: he sees that his friends will be with him in the venture, *and* he loves Dorothy. We trust ourselves in our fears when we feel or are accompanied by those who love us. We also trust ourselves when we remember we love someone who will benefit from our not being stopped by our fears. Simply recalling someone we love can thus build our trust in ourselves, as it did for Lion. Such trust is the same as letting go of fear. Being loved and loving creates a sense of our own worth that feels like confidence and well-being—what are referred to as our inner resources. Shakespeare's Romeo is also an example of how love grants freedom from fear. When he scales the high stone wall to enter Juliet's garden, she warns him of the danger of her kinsmen's apprehending him as an intruder. Romeo proclaims that death no longer matters because he can trust her love. Fear has been canceled by love, which has become more valuable than life:

> With love's light wings did I o'er-perch these walls;
> For stony limits cannot hold love out,
> And what love can do, that dares love attempt;
> Therefore thy kinsmen are no stop to me. . . .
> And but thou love me, let them find me here:
> My life were better ended by their hate,
> Than death prorogued, wanting of thy love.

Practice

FREEING OURSELVES FROM THE FEAR OF TRUSTING OUR OWN POWER

Consider whether you have ever said this to yourself:

> I might not be loved if I show my own power,
> so I choose not to claim it.

This is the same as making the choice not to love ourselves. We are, in effect, abandoning ourselves, which further decreases our power and our self-esteem.

We can begin to release ourselves from fears of all kinds by dealing directly with our fear of our own power. We can instead say to ourselves:

I accept and cherish my own power.
I am the one who has the power; fear does not have power over me. Fear has only the power I give it.
I love the big space that opens when I am free from the search for footholds, free from the fear of not finding them.

When we were not allowed to have power in childhood—that is, denied our rightful A of allowing—two long-lasting results can occur. First, we might, early on, have turned to control as an alternative. Control is the poor man's version of power. We try to gain some sense of power by controlling our environment or other people. Control arises from compulsion and increases our fear; true power arises from self-trust and increases our self-esteem. Second, we might have ongoing problems with authority, be it dealing with the supervisor at work or paying our taxes. This may be our way of getting back at our authoritarian dad. Unfortunately, such impotent rage only works against us, and we wind up with less power than ever, with the result that we are *still obeying* our father who told us we were to have no power!

You can find help in freeing yourself from fear of your own power by taking actions such as these:

- Admit you are afraid of your own power and affirm your right to have power.
- Let go of trying to control what others do or what happens to you. As long as I still can't surrender control, pistol-packing fear remains on sentry duty to make sure I do not move or move on.

- Do what is motivated by choice while still fulfilling reasonable and necessary obligations.
- Do something each day that enacts and reflects your own deepest needs, values, and wishes.
- Show your feelings as they happen.
- Speak up for yourself.
- Ask for what you want.
- Take responsibility for your behavior.
- Don't put up with abuse of any kind.
- State and maintain your boundaries, especially about the level of energy you can handle being around or taking in.
- Give up designing your behavior with the motivation of being liked.
- Do what makes you happy, not only what has redeeming value for others.
- Instead of doing only what is tried and true, be an explorer. Be open to the unknown by inserting into your daily routine something new and creative, especially if it is something out of character for you. The call to the hero is always into the unknown. Only in that "palace of dim night"—to quote Romeo—is the fulfillment of a heroic destiny possible.
- Release your intuitive and instinctive nature rather than having to be totally rational and in control at all times. This means acting in spontaneous, unguarded, natural ways—for example, engaging in demanding sports, experimenting in sexuality and sensuality—without being irresponsible.

Regarding freeing our instinctive nature, Carl Rogers, in *A Way of Being,* has a striking comment: "When I can relax and be close to the transcendental core of me, then I may behave in strange and impulsive ways in the relationship, ways which I cannot justify rationally. . . . But these strange behaviors turn out to be right, in some odd way." Here we see the connection between becoming more spiritually conscious and freeing up our animal nature. The "transcendental core" is not the opposite of our body and its release of inhibition; it is its provocateur and complement. Our earthy animal nature is called to spirituality like all the rest of our body/mind.

Nature is a brilliant ally in releasing our instincts. This happens when we enjoy the beauty of nature or when we engage in active sports in nature—for instance, river rafting or rock climbing. All this leads to a trust of ourselves in nature.

Trusting in nature, like trusting in a higher power, does not mean confidence that we will be safe from danger, injury, or death. Our trust is in the opportunity for a personally enriching contact: if we respect nature and prepare ourselves wisely to deal with its vicissitudes, we will find a lively energy in the natural world that becomes an enlivening energy in ourselves. Gerard Manley Hopkins called this energy "the dearest freshness deep down things." That ever-fresh liveliness in nature turns out to be the same as our own nature and that of a higher power too, so our experience of oneness is confirmed.

> *Every little pine needle expanded and swelled with*
> *sympathy and befriended me. I was so distinctly made*
> *aware of the presence of something kindred to me, that*
> *I thought no place could ever be strange to me again.*
> —HENRY DAVID THOREAU, *WALDEN*

When Our Story Gets in the Way

Most of us notice that there are two kinds of suffering. First there is the suffering that we can't avoid in life: all of us are touched by sickness and loss, for example. But we sometimes tack on a "do-it-yourself" kind of pain to the natural, unavoidable suffering of life. At the ending of a relationship, for instance, we might say to ourselves, "No one will ever want me now." Stories like that are fictions, superstitions we create to explain reality with labels pasted on us by our worst fears. They register in our body and make us tight and stressed, and so our body and our health often end up paying for our neurosis.

However, when we experience our real feelings purely, we are being mindful, and we are freeing ourselves from "do-it-*to*-yourself" suffering. Then our body, rather than being harmed, can help us unhook from our invented, self-destructive story line.

We can be easily seduced by a story. The fact that it is familiar makes us feel safe and secure. As we become healthier, mindfulness becomes more familiar than our patterns and stories, another reason it needs to be a daily practice.

"She does not want to be with me anymore." We can accept that as a fact without adding a story, such as: "I am unworthy; nobody really wants to be with me for very long, and this has been going on all the way back to my childhood." This story line really says, "I will hurt myself by inner put-downs because she hurt me. So first I am others' victim, and then I become my own persecutor."

Compare that self-negating style to a bare-bones affirmation of reality:

This is her decision.
I don't like it.
It has to be OK with me, and no one is wrong.
My work is to feel my sadness, anger, and any other feelings that have been evoked by this event.

When we take this approach, we begin with fact and move into feeling.

Anything can be handled in that combination of feeling and common sense once the self-defeating story lines are edited out. Paradoxically, we grow in self-trust through such whole-hearted acceptance of the reality of others. We learn to trust ourselves more because we let go of the need to trust that others will fulfill our needs in the ways we demand.

We may also notice that the list above is matter-of-fact and lacks the entertainment value of the dramatic story we invent. Could it be that our stories are a skewed way of entertaining ourselves? The challenge for an adult is to seek entertainment at the movies, not in events that call for work on ourselves.

An alternative way of handling the fact that others may not fulfill us as we want them to is egotistical indifference: "The hell with them." This is a form of despair that attempts to salve our wounded ego. It is not a skillful means toward health in relationships. Such despair contrasts with spiritually mature indifference: "Some people will really like me and some won't, *and I wish them all well*." This is getting on with our life with loving-kindness rather than getting stuck in a story about our life. We really can trust ourselves to handle people's not wanting to be with us as much as we want them to without adding any story about them or us. Self-confidence is freedom from the need for a story. *Then our commitment to being healthy and acting with integrity becomes more valuable than whether everyone or anyone wants us.*

Practice

ERASING THE STORYBOARD

Mindfulness, a central Buddhist practice in meditation and in daily life, means that we keep coming back to the here and now, to pure experience uncluttered by mental chatter. Attention to our breath helps us to focus in that way. Mindfulness is a spiritual practice that liberates us into the authentic present by awakening us to how our mind distracts us with fear, desire, judgment, attachment, comparison, bias, and attempts to control what happens around us.

We sit quietly and keep returning to our breath as a reminder to be present in the here and now. Events, such as thoughts, are experienced purely when we do not fixate on them, reject them, or add to them. The add-ons, such as fear, blame/shame, escape, judgment, and attempts to fix and control, are the smoke and mirrors that distract us from reality.

Here is a way of working with the add-ons, the distracting and entertaining mind-sets that charge up our thoughts, feelings, and experiences. We begin with a simple example:

Fact: I Realize That I Will Die Someday

- I worry about when it will happen. (Fear is add-on one.)
- I blame myself for worrying. I should be above all that. (Blame is add-on two.)
- I try to escape the thought altogether. (Escape is add-on three.)
- I notice that I'm not able to stop worrying about this, that I cannot escape it, and I judge myself as inadequate. (Judgment is add-on four. This harsh verdict is pronounced by our inner "hanging judge," who is hard as nails. When we judge ourselves as wrong, we also feel we are in danger of being punished, so fear follows on the heels of self-judgment, and this strengthens the fear add-on.)
- I look for some way around the fact. For example, I get involved in planning to exercise more and take vitamin supplements to extend my life. (Fixing/controlling is add-on five.)

The five additions constitute my homemade sufferings. They are my futile stabs at avoiding the appropriate pain in the pure fact, the given that I will someday die. That pain is grief, something we do not want to feel, and so we buffer it with add-ons, each a story line too. Now we see why a yes to the givens of life is so healthy. We are staying with our own reality. We are facing our feelings and working them through directly. The spiritual practice of mindfulness helps us get there. Our mindfulness practice is not a way to avoid feeling, only to experience it without the ego's usual elaborations.

With mindfulness, the same situation looks like this:

Fact: I Realize That I Will Die

- I drop any story lines that start to emerge by attention to my breathing, by staying still, and by opening to my feelings. These may include sadness, a sense of protest, and a desire to escape. But I don't try to run away from all this, I stay with it. This is how I notice the way my body feels, and I stay with my emotions.

- My feelings are pure rather than ego-generated. I show myself the five A's: attention, acceptance, affection, appreciation, and allowing.

- After staying with my feelings for a while, I find that I begin to accept death as the common fate of humanity.

- I can now be aware of death but not possessed by any of my habitual add-ons that turn it into a phobia or an obsession.

With mindfulness, my sense of grief about death turns into acceptance, and that leads to equanimity, a source of quiet joy. *Then I am no longer the one stuck. I am the one who has started to get unstuck.* This is how change—and greater self-trust—begins to happen.

We are no longer under the influence of add-ons, ego mind-sets, story lines, superstitions. Our sense of self becomes porous because it is no longer so defended. We have accepted impermanence in body and mind, a great step toward seeing death, or anything, as a fact. Mindfulness grants us a vision of impermanence, since we are carefully witnessing the ever-moving train of thought and our reactions to each of its cars, engine to caboose. Mindfulness is thus the opposite of obsession.

In mindfulness, we also disidentify with our story of fear and desire as well as all the other flotsam that makes life's voyage so complicated. Then we relate to what happens rather than oppose it. We may notice three wonderful results:

1. As we remain present to what is without complaint or blame, we say, and become, a yes to here-and-now reality. This leads us to trust reality.

2. As we stay with what is, with no story lines, our present moment is pure awareness, no longer trammeled by mind-sets. This is because mind-sets produce the charge we have around something. When mind-sets go, we can trust ourselves because we are no longer in bondage to our jittery ego. We are re-located in our own power. Ralph Waldo Emerson expressed it well: "When half gods go, the gods arrive."

3. As we awaken the qualities of enlightenment in ourselves, we become channels for universal and unconditional love, the wisdom of the ages, and an ever-lively healing. This leads us to trust our wholeness, now and ever in us.

Write in your journal using the style of the example above. At the top of a new page, identify a fact in your own life that you have been struggling with.

Ask yourself what your specific add-ons have been (fear, blame, escape, judgment).

After each of your add-ons, look back to the top of the page at the fact itself and mindfully open yourself to the pure experience of it.

Notice what the feeling or issue is like without your added story lines.

Notice as you do this how much freer you feel.

Practices such as these can help us face ourselves and our feelings in a kinder way, and this endows us with a power far beyond any reward we were getting from our ego. The more we take a chance on trusting ourselves and others, the more others open up to us and become trustworthy toward us.

5

Trust Lost,
Trust Regained

DANTE PLACED JUDAS AND BRUTUS in the lowest circle of hell to show that betrayal is the worst of sins. We are hurt most deeply when those we trust turn against us. The loss of trust takes more than grief to get over. It is shocking, isolating, and disorienting. Our challenge is to reconstitute our whole perspective on ourselves, on others, and on humanity. We have to restabilize ourselves in our familiar world, no easy task. A breakdown in trust requires personal work on our part too. We are challenged to revisit similar hurts from the past and grieve them along with grieving the hurt that just occurred.

How does betrayal happen to us? Trust is undermined when someone is unfaithful to us; deceives us; cheats us; lies to us; turns on us; acts unilaterally; shows malice toward us; gossips about us unfairly; makes a big decision without talking to us about it beforehand; takes advantage of our vulnerability; breaks our confidence; doesn't come through for us; runs from our feelings; isn't there for us in a crisis; doesn't check in with us when we are in distress; says no to addressing, processing, and resolving our mutual conflicts.

One of the reasons it is such a risk to trust our fellow humans is that we know so well that there is no limit to human aggression. Some other animals, when fighting, pull back when the opponent shows his throat in surrender, out of an instinct for species preservation. We humans might keep attacking. We have to be taught to stop or be stopped by someone. This is why growing in personal integrity contributes to our collective survival. In any case, we always have it in us to work on our own aggressive instincts and make a commitment to act with nonviolent love in all our dealings. To make that commitment increases our trust in the enlightened potential in ourselves and others.

In friendship and relationship, trust grows when we find safety to express our authentic feelings. Trust is broken when we are shut down or punished for our feelings. Can we trust this friend or partner with such feelings as anger, sadness, or fear? There are two possibilities: Some people easily welcome our sharing our feelings about others. This is the friend who, for instance, remains very present to us as we describe and express what we feel about our spouse. However, that same friend may not be open to hearing our feelings when they are directed toward himself. Then he may become testy or defensive rather than welcoming. When we give him feedback about that reaction, he becomes even more defensive, refusing to address the breakdown of communication. We try once more later, but still no luck.

When this happens, we do not reject him, only recognize his inhibitions about accepting feedback. The challenge for us is to trade in our fantasy about how open we thought he was for the reality of who he actually is. Our level of trust has been reduced and reproportioned. So we may have to switch to small talk and cut back on our time together. This is the response of mindfulness and loving-kindness. Mindfully, we are staying with the reality of who someone is without judgment or blame. In loving-kindness we are not rejecting or retaliating but still holding him in our circle of love.

Trust does not have to end the way a bear dies, impossible to resuscitate. It can end the way a bear hibernates, able to be re-animated given the right conditions and a suitable lapse of time. Trust can begin to be restored when the untrustworthy person apologizes and offers to make amends. Then a long, consistent history of trustworthiness has to follow for us to trust again with confidence, something that happens only gradually, a feature of all grief and reorientation.

There are people who have caused pain to themselves and others by their addictions, compulsions, or crimes. When they find recovery or "get religion" they may expect others to trust them instantly. This is more than an unreasonable demand. It is an illusion often found in conversion experiences: "Now that I am a new person, I have no shadow, no negative side. Before I was totally untrustworthy but now I am totally reliable." Recovery, transformation, change, and conversion all require on-going acknowledgment of the shadow side that remains in us no matter how much better we look, feel, and act. In authentic transformation, we remain aware of how unconscious forces of aggression are in all of us. It takes daily discipline to work with the negative impulses that are in no way cancelled by being "born again."

The Silent Treatment

Mutuality in a relationship builds trust between partners. In adult relationships, sudden unilateral silence or an abrupt disappearance impairs our ability to trust. This is because it is directly opposed to our addressing, processing, resolving, and integrating our problems together. Arbitrary decision making signals a lack of trust from one partner to another.

Someone's unexplained rejection of us leaves us with so many questions, including what *we* did wrong. Consider a second kind of experience. We are told directly by a partner that things are not working and why. This partner offers to work things out or to be with us as we work out our feelings about the breakup.

In the first instance, our pain is happening because we are being wounded at the trust level, the heart level, the most delicate part of us. The grief is saturated with betrayal, perhaps reminiscent of past hurts, and will take a while to be worked through. In the second instance, our partner is willing to address the issue, showing integrity. She is respecting our feelings with her willingness to see them through. She is not jumping ship but staying on board with us to the next harbor.

No one can infallibly promise permanence in a relationship, since feelings change. But an adult with integrity can say that though he can't be relied on never to go, he will be relied on not to run. Everyone can be trustworthy in that way.

An example of a unilateral style, a favorite entitlement of ego, is the silent treatment, an aggressive and vindictive style in a relationship, a form of pouting. In the early phase of a relationship, such distancing can arise from fear, ego's first name. For instance, Barry is afraid of the closeness happening in his new relationship, so he suddenly ceases contact with Madelyn. Wondering what is going on, she calls and e-mails Barry, but there is no response. Madelyn is wondering what she did wrong. Then she gets angry and wants to be sarcastic. In those phases, she is wise not to contact Barry. For one thing, she does not know for sure what is happening. He may be in the hospital in a coma. (This is unlikely, since bad news gets back to us easily.) Second, Madelyn might say something inappropriate that she will regret later because it was not in keeping with her loving-kindness practice.

Madelyn will wait to calm down and then send one last e-mail to Barry, saying, "I haven't heard from you and hope everything is all right." She does not say, "I hope we are all right," because that presumes a "we," and that may no longer be the case. Madelyn is hurting, and Barry *knows* that. His use of the silent treatment shows that her pain is not as important as his own self-protection. That is important information about Barry for Madelyn, especially early on in the relationship. It shows that he has work to do on his ego before he can participate in a healthy intimate bond with anyone. Madelyn remembers that she is in the investigatory phase of the relationship. On one level, Madelyn is glad that she is finding out more about someone she was considering as a prospective partner.

In any case, unilateral silence is a clear indication that Barry cannot be trusted. Hopefully, Madelyn will maintain her own self-respect and make no further inquiries or entreaties but let the chips fall where they may. When and if Barry does call and wants to resuscitate the relationship, Madelyn will need to ask for a full explanation, explore the fact that he knew she was hurting and did not make a simple phone call to ease her pain, and finally make an agreement that Barry drop the silent treatment permanently. Trust grows in a relationship when we can say directly to a partner, "I will never use the silent treatment or retaliation," and when we can commit ourselves to following through with it.

Madelyn may prefer simply to say good-bye. It's not necessary for her to risk more with Barry. Her free speech, delivered without concern for the outcome, and her fortifying her own boundaries build Madelyn's trust in herself. Maybe that will mean more to her than finding a man.

Here is another example of unilateral silence, this time in the early dating phase. We have some wonderful evenings with someone new. She promises to contact us soon. Then we never hear from her again. We speculate that this prospective partner had second thoughts or cold feet. Those mentally generated explanations do not harm us. When we add on story lines, telling ourselves that she found someone better, realized we had nothing to offer, or saw through us, we damage our self-esteem. In reality, the lack of follow-through tells us only that the other person is someone who does not follow through. She does not want to continue the relationship, which is her right, and she does not choose to let us know—not very polite, but there it is.

Our reaction to silence may take one of the three forms we explored earlier: reaching out, anger, or despair. We may keep reaching out to the other person no matter what. This violates the boundaries of the silent person, who has made it clear that she does not welcome further contact. It can also indicate a willingness to let ourselves be hurt by the other's rejection, over and over.

We may simply remain angry until it becomes a bitterness that can lead to depression. In addition, our ability to trust diminishes when we are depressed because an effect of depression is that nothing seems *reliable*. This too makes us agents of our own homemade suffering. It is also contrary to a yes to the given that no relationship is possible with this person and it is up to us to move on to grieving and to let go of blame. This will take an embracing of vulnerability, the quality that we may believe got us into this trouble to begin with.

We can distinguish the silent treatment from a time-out. Our silence then is not aggressive. It is the normal time it takes to understand and feel through an experience or idea. In this instance, we might say to at partner: "Give me some time to be with this on my own." We then resume communication as soon as we have a clearer picture of what we really feel and need. The silence is meant to clarify not to punish.

Finally, Buddhist writer Stephen T. Butterfield wrote of a positive dimension in betrayal that is not to be overlooked: "Since no relationship can be made entirely safe and secure . . . this has to mean trust in one's own ability to use any consequence, including betrayal, as a means for waking up." Thus, the spiritually conscious person might take a breach of trust as a teaching about the given of life that anyone can bolt from us with no explanation, another reminder of impermanence.

We should be careful to get out of an experience only the wisdom that is in it and stop there; lest we be like the cat that sits down on a hot stove-lid. She will never sit down on a hot stove-lid again and that is well; but also she will never sit down on a cold one anymore.
—MARK TWAIN, *PUDD'NHEAD WILSON'S NEW CALENDAR, FOLLOWING THE EQUATOR, 1897*

Lies We Tell, Hear, or Won't Hear

In an episode of the TV sitcom *All in the Family,* Archie Bunker is disappointed with his wife, Edith, because she would not lie to gain the family some money. Archie chastises Edith, saying, "I'm talking about families sticking together."

Edith, in her characteristically naive yet profound way, replies, "Oh, Archie, I believe in families sticking together, but if I hadn't told the truth, you'd never be able to trust me again. And then how could we stick together?"

"Archie" and "Edith" may represent two sides of ourselves.

Deep down we believe it is wrong to lie, in that it breaks the bond of human trust. At the same time, our need, fear, or greed may make it seem all right to take liberties with the truth. We lie for a number of different reasons:

To get what we want
To keep a secret
To hide the truth
To protect our body, possessions, or turf
To save ourselves from embarrassment
To preserve our image
To avoid further inquiry
To justify our behavior
To avoid a responsibility
To avoid conflict (or conflict resolution)
To preserve the status quo
To inflate our ego
To hide our feelings
To manipulate someone
To make a fool of someone
To get back at someone who has lied to us

Notice that these reasons are all fear-based. When we are afraid, we may seek refuge in lying rather than in being forthcoming. Unlike Gandhi, we do not trust in the power of truth as much as we do in our own version of what works.

Once we see the connection between lying and fear, we begin to understand why trust and truth have to go hand in hand. Trust requires an ongoing commitment to truthfulness in communication. Yet communication can include lying. However, *communion* does not. In that trusted bond, we feel safe to share the truth about ourselves. This is why trust and truth can happen only in a relationship of authentic intimacy.

Lying about oneself or one's actions undermines trust. Being truthful stabilizes trust. As we have seen, trust means that we do not fear the one we trust. If we believe we have to lie in order to feel safe and secure, we are not in the ballpark of trust.

Honest self-presentation is actually built into us biologically. The muscles of our face are geared to portray in exact detail every mood and feeling we are having. This happens without conscious thought. So when we hide our truth, we are overriding a natural tendency. Our body wants to tell the truth. Our fear wants to cover it up.

We can distinguish honesty from self-disclosure. A trustworthy person is always honest but is not necessarily self-revealing to everyone. His sense of boundaries includes keeping some information about himself private. In fact, at times he may be obliged to do this—as in maintaining confidentiality. As wise adults, we are unconditionally honest in our dealings and conditionally self-disclosing. We are unconditionally honest in our speech and conditional about what we choose to reveal.

For instance, in loving-kindness, our honest opinion of others has to be seasoned with compassion. We tell as much of our truth as we imagine they can handle and in as kind a way as possible. Here we face conflicting imperatives. One rule is to be honest, and another is to be kind. It is not a struggle between good and evil but between good and good. When we keep practicing loving-kindness, we always know which path to choose.

Some people lie to their partners about their past, what they did and with whom, as, for example, in the film *Deception*. Some partners lie about their present feelings. They may not tell us what is positive about us, such as how much we mean to them. They may hide what is negative, such as the fact that for them the thrill in the relationship is gone, that someone else has captured their fancy, that they are leaving tomorrow. Some partners lie about the future. They promise us the moon but have no intention of giving it to us. They vow fidelity but secretly retain the right to break that vow if someone better comes along. Their fidelity is contingent on their options.

That secret holdout shows the primacy of "me" over "us." Those who hold out without telling us may feel that it is legitimate to do so. They may believe it is a needed protection of their liberty, something to which they are entitled. Trustworthiness toward a partner is secondary to their own needs and therefore not of great value to them. A truly trustworthy person has become mature enough not to be fickle. He gives up the chance of getting immediate gratification from a better offer that has come along. He has become willing to subordinate his own pleasure to the tremendous value of an enduring commitment. This is what is meant by true fidelity.

It is hard to know whether someone is a liar unless he slips up and gives us a clue. But there are people we trust implicitly and rightly so. There are also people we never quite trust, though we have no specific evidence, just an intuitive sense about them. That doubt will not be acceptable very long in a healthy adult relationship. The one with the doubts will want to address the issue until suspicions are laid to rest. It is important to check out our doubts, to say out loud that we are having them. We can usually tell by the response, especially if it is defensive and blustering, whether we have hit a nerve. By the way, the ability to lie to someone's face and look sincere is not a talent but a major and tragic deficit in the ongoing enterprise of human relating. Not to be embarrassed or ashamed of oneself (healthy shame) for lying is a clear sign of untrustworthiness.

It is rare for a person to lie only once. People who lie to us are usually doing it in a variety of areas. Some people lie automatically in order to prevent others from seeing what's really going on. Addicts lie repeatedly to protect their addiction, for example. As we have been seeing, integrity is always the best indicator of trustworthiness. We can trust that we are with someone who tells the truth by noticing her standards with people across the board. If she lies, cheats, steals in the wider world, she is most likely doing it with us. If her life program involves a commitment to integrity, honesty, and loving-kindness in all her dealings, we can trust her to be that way with us.

Humans have become quite adept at concealing. A boy walks to school every day from kindergarten to twelfth grade with his best friend. He has been beaten by his mother this morning or last night, and he does remember it but he will not tell. He does not discuss it even with his own brother, who has also been beaten. He could have told the story of his pain and asked for comforting. Most of us boys were so repressed we could not chance asking for the five A's from a male friend, lest he think we were weak or perhaps coming on to him. We learned early to trust our fear more than our right to ask for support.

We also had to hide the violence done to us because we did not want to be seen as victims, an image not compatible with being a "man" in our society. Instead, we kept up appearances, covering up our pain and the violence of others toward us. How sadly ironic, since that is precisely how we remain victimized.

The boy in this example is not really lying to his friend, only not self-disclosing. He is protecting his mother's image and his own embarrassing victimization. In that sense, he is lying to himself. In addition, society lied to him when it said that males are not allowed to be victims, only heroes; not to have needs, only solutions. The path to changing that in adult life is in admitting our wounds to someone we trust, asking for support, and grieving our childhood experience.

If our habit is lying within an adult relationship in order to maintain our own self-centered purposes, our work is not grief but direct change through a commitment to truthfulness. The tools of psychology or psychotherapy alone won't get us there.

This may require a spiritual program. Once we develop our spiritual consciousness, our commitment is to appearing as we are rather than having to look good at all times, telling the truth about ourselves even when it is embarrassing, expressing our appropriate feelings as they arise, asserting our needs no matter how vulnerable they make us look. When we live by such standards as those, we can trust ourselves to be truthful rather than caught in the default setting of lying-to-protect. It is only when there is no longer anything to protect that lies can yield to honest self-presentation. We recall Janis Joplin singing, "Freedom's just another word for nothing left to lose."

We are sometimes lying to ourselves in subtle ways: we might deny when and how we need help, what our real needs are, what addictions we are caught in, how much or even whether we really love those we say we do. These lies also originate in fear. We are afraid of the challenge underlying each one. We stop lying to ourselves when we admit to ourselves and someone we trust who we really are, with all our shortcomings. Lies thrive in an atmosphere of isolation. This is why having a trustworthy support system makes it easier to be honest.

When we lie to others, we are cheating ourselves. Getting what we want has become more important than maintaining our integrity. We lower our opinion of ourselves because we know that we are liars. That causes a dangerous erosion of our self-esteem. We cheat ourselves and lose our self-respect.

It is intriguing and curious, by the way, that lies figure into the stories of the origin of most religions and become useful teachings. In Judaism, Jacob lies to his father by masquerading as Esau to steal his brother's inheritance. In Christianity, Peter lies three times about knowing Jesus. The Buddha's father lied to his son about the world, protecting him from knowing there were such realities as sickness, old age, and death. Krishna, in one interpretation of the story, lies to the goatherdesses, telling each of them that she is the only one for him, as he secretly engages in sex with all of them, by turns.

All four of these lies are based on fear and the desire to protect. Jacob is afraid to miss out on an inheritance and wants to advance his own offspring. Peter is afraid of being arrested and lies to protect his life. The Buddha's father feared that his son might be saddened by the givens of life, so he tried to protect him from them. Perhaps Krishna lies for fear of not experiencing all the women and to protect his image as faithful in each of their opinions.

In each instance, the lie is a teaching device that opens us to a transcendent truth. Jacob's lie shows how an unethical act can lead to a mystical journey. Peter's lie shows the power of fear and the force of repentance. The Buddha discovers the reality of suffering, and that leads to his enlightenment and to teaching us how to find freedom. Krishna is the trickster whose lie reveals to us the folly of believing in special entitlements.

Now our challenge is to learn all that from the truth just as it is. Gandhi is our model, since he believed in the power of truth and was willing to put his life on the line for it. He could do this because his protest had no aggressive charge attached to it. Gandhi could believe fervently but keep his focus on the action, his spiritual practice, which does away with every mind-set, every ego wish to hit back, every ego fear to turn back. We have that same pure potential for trusting in truth. The path to that trust is telling the truth, which is also the path to trusting ourselves.

A Double Life

Some people seem cut out for a steady, monogamous relationship, staying close to hearth and home. They like spending most of their time in the company of a partner and family, having a home together, and being householders. Others like having relationships but seem not to be cut out for staying put. They prefer to keep fires going in a variety of places. They may have another partner somewhere, a wanderlust, or other fascinations that take them away for long periods. They may not want a special someone. But they do want one person they can keep coming back to.

Any of these styles can work if it is mutually acceptable. This means that each person is willing to be honest about his or her agenda and has no secret sideline. One person may say, "I want to settle down and get married and live with you and be faithful to you." Another may say, "I want to be free to come and go, not be married, have an open relationship, but remain connected to you as my home-base person." Whatever adults choose to do with their eyes wide open can work as long as there is honesty and a willingness to engage in the extra work it takes to keep the relationship afloat.

The problems begin when someone says he wants to settle down but secretly plans to wander, another form of the unilateral style. This is secrecy as a form of lying, a violation of trust. The partner at home may never doubt the other person, in which case her trust is a mistake. Or she may live in doubt, never knowing for sure what the other is up to, while continually looking for clues. Trust is not viable in either example, nor is intimate relating happening.

A central feature of a trustworthy commitment is keeping agreements. A partner who is leading a double life cannot offer that. A secret life refers to a parallel existence in which someone is engaging in another relationship, an addiction, or another set of behaviors, known only to himself. This can take the form of having an affair or having one or more partners or families in other towns. It may also be a sex addiction, such as to pornography, frequenting of strip clubs or prostitutes. It may involve an alternative lifestyle, such as a sexual orientation not in keeping with what someone says is his. The addiction can also be to gambling, alcohol, or drugs.

An irony appears in the choice of a double life. Usually, the one who engages in secrecy seeks to keep the focus of a partner or family away from himself. Yet, by his lifestyle, he actually draws attention to himself. That is an example of the human comedy at work: we do what is meant to protect us from scrutiny and thereby draw it to ourselves more emphatically.

People who engage in a double life usually do not see what they do as breaking trust with the other person. They believe, or rationalize, that they have certain needs that their partner cannot fully understand and should not be required to fulfill. They rationalize that they can find their own private satisfaction of these needs without harm to their primary relationship. They might not want to upset their stable life at home by letting the truth come out. They might be ashamed or afraid to let their needs be known. They might believe they are "only experimenting" and that justifies their behavior.

Surreptitiousness is the style of a double life. We are purposely misleading our partner. Our motive is not to protect our inner core, as it is in legitimate secrecy, but rather trying to appear one way and act in another. This is why a secret life that is meant to deceive a partner lacks integrity. We are giving the impression that we are maintaining a bond when in truth we're not.

Some people enjoy the success of their deception because it means they have fooled others. However, gaining a sense of power and satisfaction by getting away with something, pulling the wool over someone's eyes, is a sign of immaturity. A mature adult will not find pleasure or power in trickery or sham but in sharing, in coming forward, in affirming an identity rather than masking it.

The partner who is being deceived may be truly in the dark. She may also be aware that something is afoot but choose not to inquire into it. She may be afraid to know, or simply not interested in knowing, as long as she has a minimally or generally satisfying or at least nonabusive relationship with her partner.

Some partners lead a double life but not a secret life. They tell their partners openly about their choice to engage in extracurricular activities. The other partner can then decide how to respond. One person may find it a deal-breaker. Another may choose to go along with the program but not to be told of the details. She may take similar action and begin a double life as well. It is also possible that a deeply revealing conversation about the plan for a double life can be so satisfying and illuminating that it does not have to be acted on after all! It is up to each couple to plan their style, but honesty at each step of the way is necessary if there is to be any level of trust.

An unrevealed, surreptitious life certainly contains its own brand of excitement, an adrenaline rush that is a major feature of the enjoyment. The ancient Greek poet Pindar wrote, "Secrecy has added pleasure to the activity." The surreptitious style of a double life makes for thrills not to be found in ordinary relating. Committed adults will not be captivated by that enticement, though they will not deny the appeal of the sirens' lay.

Practice

LETTING GO OF OBSESSION

We may be quite comfortable at home by the hearth, but we are in love with someone who is happier being Peter Pan. We then might become obsessed with the idea of getting him to stay put, wondering about his whereabouts, and being generally unhappy because he does not come through as we want him to. This same style can refer to any relationship in which one person wants more than what the other is willing to offer.

If we become obsessed with our Peter Pan, we give him power over us: he is now in charge of our happiness. Coins have two sides, and human coinage is no different. One side of the coin is that Peter Pan matters to us; the other side is the power we give him. One side is beyond our control; the other isn't. There is very little we can do to erase or even lessen our feelings for someone. But we can stop granting him power over us.

If you are obsessed with a partner or a potential partner, try —behave, not pretend—disempowering that person in your psyche: Act *as if* he were no longer the be-all and end-all of your life using the model for reducing ego, the FACE exercise:

Fear: Ask yourself what you are afraid of, and then affirm that where fear is, you can act with loving-kindness instead, no matter what the other person does. Recommit yourself to regular loving-kindness practice. (In this practice, do not mention him by name but include him only in a general way—for example, "May my friends be happy.")

Attachment: Say to yourself, "In each way that I am unhealthily attached to this person, I let go. I give up all my strategies to make him into what I want him to be."

Control: "Wherever I am trying to control his behavior so he will want me more, I allow him to be who he is and demand nothing more from him. I give up wishing it could be more. I now put my emphasis on how to be a good friend to myself, him, and everyone. I use healthy control to maintain my boundaries."

Entitlement: You do have a right to happiness, but you don't have the right to *demand* it from anyone. Keep asking yourself, "How can I hold this relationship so that I don't expect it to deliver something to me?"

When We Cheat

Our capacity to be faithful to someone begins to show itself in adolescence when we are loyal to friends or to a partner. Some of us lack this capacity. Then fidelity is proportional to the opportunities that come along. For instance, a person may be remaining faithful in a relationship mostly because no more attractive person has become available.

When we are in a relationship and a new person sweeps us off our feet, our excitement may be coming from him or her. However, it may also be coming from within ourselves, a mental projection of how wonderful it would be and how perfect life would become if we only had that person in our lives. Such a projection reeks with denial of the given of life that nothing stays the same for very long. Projection here refers to our wishful thinking about what something means, who someone really is, or what someone will give us and for how long.

This kind of projection is powerful for two reasons. Physically, it is fed by adrenaline, the lifeblood of addiction. Psychologically, it is fed by instinctive need. For instance, we want to be accepted as we are, and our spouse is continually criticizing us. We meet someone who does accept us unconditionally, who loves us, foibles and all. We project onto her the archetype of the perfect lover, the one who truly gets us, our soul mate. Some of the projection is reality-based, since our needs will indeed be fulfilled by this person. Some of the projection is based on a wish that our need for acceptance will be perfectly slaked at last, after too long and frustrating a thirst.

When adrenaline and projection kick in, we are sitting ducks for the drama of infidelity. The forces of thrill and desire become so overwhelming that a spouse, no matter how faultless, cannot compete with the new love interest in our lives. A familiar partner or spouse can make all the right moves but can't awaken that special chemistry that happens in an exciting new dalliance. This is because the person having the affair:

- Feels wanted, valued, desirable, and for those reasons exceedingly satisfied, no matter how objectively ordinary the whole experience may be.
- Can make his own choices and be his free-spirited self rather than fulfill the obligations of a co-parent, a household business partner, or a caretaker, as at home.
- Has nothing to prove, always measures up, does not have to look or act a certain way, is not judged by age or body shape.
- Is more relaxed at home, since he can be more patient with his partner. While being duplicitous and engaging in deceit, "It is now easier to be nice on the outside while still being angry at or indifferent toward you on the inside."
- Has noticed that time stands still during an assignation with the lover, so there is a sense of the transcendent in the air.
- Is entranced by the special intensity, fueled by the secrecy in the sexual pleasure.
- Has more permission to be uninhibited, to try new forms of pleasure, including recreational drugs, which may not be acceptable to the partner at home.
- Finds an adrenaline rush in the surreptitious planning of assignations as well as the anxiety about being found out.
- Feels the thrill of close attachment to someone who fulfills needs long unattended to.

With respect to this last point, we can notice that the ultimate motivation for most addictive bonds is a *merger* experience.

Our search for merger goes back to the symbiotic phase in infancy, when our oneness with Mother meant total safety and security. All through life, we may long for access to the ocean of mystical oneness. This is our inclination toward the transcendent. Our fear of losing contact with that power once we find it can make us possessive. That is certainly visible in romantic love in which we want so much to possess our partner. Our desire for the transcendent, combined with possessiveness, shows up in any addiction.

How ironic that we seek the permanently transcendent in addictions, which can offer it only temporarily. We seek the profound in shallow ground. This is why recovery from any addiction is ultimately a spiritual program requiring a bond with a "higher power," the healthy alternative to the merger we experience when we use drugs or alcohol. Now we have found that which is deep, not shallow; ongoing, not temporary; maturing, not infantilizing.

Regarding the "anxiety about being found out" in the list above, we notice that affairs thrive on suspense: "When and where can we next meet safely?" "Will we be caught?" "Will we ever be together permanently?" A healthy person is looking for suspense only in books and movies, not in his relationships. In adult intimacy, we seek the five A's in an atmosphere of security and safety, reciprocally provided and tranquilly reliable.

Our adult challenge is always to follow our bliss. It is also to follow and investigate our wishes, feelings, and behavior. Yet, in all this, we have to acknowledge and respect the contract we have made with our partner. It also provides us information. As we explore our infidelity and its meaning, we read our new love interest as a dramatic portrayal of what is missing in our relationship. We can choose to act with integrity and to deal directly with our partner about what is missing. Then we decide together or singly whether our primary relationship does have a future, and we take action accordingly. If we decide to work something out within our relationship, we end the affair. Only if our original relationship ends do we make ourselves available to this other person. This, of course, does not apply in "open relationships" in which the partners have agreed beforehand on a nonmonogamous lifestyle.

We know that we have become wiser when we make the transition from the need for the cloak-and-dagger adrenaline rush to the need for honesty and a decision to reconstitute the original relationship or to break up amicably. Our body confirms the sanity of our choice, since that transition will feel right all over, like the shift from a breakfast of black coffee, a doughnut, and a cigarette to a breakfast of wholesome oatmeal.

The sense of satisfaction from such a decision is not hot and heavy, but we no longer crave that anyway. Now we want contented energy, not stressful energy. This is how we know that the Don Juan archetype has finally yielded to the committed partner archetype. Now when other women appear on our horizon who look better than our spouse or offer what we see as more than we are getting at home, we take it only as information, not as a motivation to stray. Our options may be entertaining, but they are not entrancing.

Self-deception and rationalization can enable untrustworthy individuals to continue their unfaithful behavior. They may be remorseful, but only after their untrustworthy actions are disclosed. They may then profess to value the one they have hurt, but this may be to avoid the consequences of loss of home, family, and lifestyle. Remorse is sorrow about one's offenses. Repentance is sorrow with a sincere desire to make amends and to amend one's life. A person who is untrustworthy may feel remorse but not repentance.

A deceptive partner might never have felt an obligation to be trustworthy. This is a form of sociopathy in which untrustworthiness—or even crime—is allowed and not considered immoral or unfair. The perpetrator feels that he or she is above the rules of fair play but would not tolerate being treated in that same way.

A sociopath is a person with no guilt or sense of loyalty. He is distinguished from the psychopath, who is, in addition, violent and dangerous to society. Any person may cope with stress by numbing his own feelings and thereby losing his empathy for others' pain.

We all have the potential to act in sociopathic ways. The imperial ego can make us believe we need not follow the same rules that others do. Our untrustworthiness, we think, does not count against us because we are more intelligent or more evolved than others. We believe ourselves entitled to special privileges in relationships and in life in general. We believe that our needs are highly complex and unique, so only we can decide how they are to be satisfied. In this mind-set, we deceive others about our needs and plans to avoid interference or interruption.

When We Are Betrayed

The breakdown of trust in a relationship is a much more hurtful moment than the breakup of the relationship. To be betrayed inflicts a deep wound that takes a long time to get over. We feel alone—that is, we feel we have no one to trust. This makes our pain so piercing. Our partner, no matter how repentant, can help but can't really get us through it. Only time and work on ourselves can make a difference. The work is grieving the loss of an uncomplicated connection with our partner—and of our own innocence.

We who are betrayed are confronting a radically adult choice. We can follow the well-trodden path of lamenting our woebegone state, sinking into self-pity and despair, or licking our ego's wounds by nursing blame, hatred, and plans for revenge. (In all these cases, our physical and psychological health are likely to suffer.)

Or we can choose a path of courage and compassion: we can feel our grief and let our feelings of sadness, anger, and fear lead us to examine our past and how similar betrayals happened to us before. As we stay with our feelings without blame or the need to retaliate, we are healing ourselves and acting with integrity. Then a path can open for us to finish some of our unfinished business from former relationships and to get on with our life, with or without a partner.

As we heal, we rejoice in how much lighter we feel with fewer illusions. That joy is worth so much more than continuing the sham of shelter and security. After all, our life purpose was always about evolving from narrow ego safety into an enlightened openness. And this is helping us get there, albeit kicking and screaming—but there's no shame in that.

Part of the reason that being left by someone is so difficult is that it is not only a loss or betrayal. We notice when we are left by someone that three archetypes come to roost in our lives: the orphan, the freed slave, and the hero. We feel abandoned, which brings in the orphan archetype. We are released from being with someone who is not really into us, which connects us to the archetype of the freed slave. Finally, the pain we feel is initiatory—that is, it makes us strong enough to face whatever other dragons may come along. Now we are in the hero archetype.

These three archetypal energies happening all at once make the experience somewhat incoherent. Yet they are enormously useful to our growth when we become conscious of them and work with each to gain both its benefits and its graces. The orphan archetype offers us the opportunity to stand alone and survive that way. The freed slave makes room for us to move on in our own life and make new choices that more adequately fit our needs and desires. The hero archetype is about empowerment, so what has happened readies us for whatever challenge may next arise. In addition, making friends with these three energies in our deep self increases our lively energy. This is just what we need to get on with life.

In any ending forced upon us, a spiritual opportunity has also arisen. Every betrayal in a relationship challenges our belief in permanence and our entitlement to fidelity. Being left by a partner who has found someone new is certainly an excruciating way to learn those truths. But from the point of view of spiritual awakening, infidelity toward us is a wake-up call, helping us dismantle our ego. When we realize that promises made to us will not necessarily be kept just because we are who we are, we are finding a path to humility. When we realize that our safe house was only a house of cards, we are being graced with a chance to release ourselves from fantasy in favor of the truth. We may notice that when we are attached to a fantasy and someone brings us down to earth, we will feel as if he took something from us. This adds to our sadness and anger, which helps us grieve more effectively.

When we realize that our wishes don't matter to the one who has abandoned us, we are being given the gift of freedom from our childish holdouts from the givens of adult life. This blow to our sense of specialness, this feeling of not being valued, this kick in the teeth—none of this is fun, deserved, or desirable. But this *is* an opportunity for the practice of letting go of ego entitlement and illusion. Betrayal hurts but does not have to harm, not any more than the surgeon harms us with her scalpel. Imagine giving ego-dismantling such priority that we might even welcome the chance to let it happen! When we are faced with betrayal, these verses from the poet Rumi encourage us to focus on letting go of ego rather than strategizing:

> Don't keep trying to find new ways to
> move across the chessboard.
> Listen for when the word "checkmate"
> will be directed at you.

Why We Put Up with Pain

When there is a breakdown of trust, we wonder why sometimes the betrayed or abused partner tolerates unhappiness and hurt for quite a while rather than taking expeditious action to make a change. It is a mystery about us humans that we will sometimes act or persist in self-defeating ways:

We may undermine our chances for fulfillment or contentment.

We may be drawn easily into situations in which we will suffer, as in a relationship in which we know that our partner strays.

We may stay in such a relationship for a lifetime. When others offer to help us, we may say no.

We may stay in relationships characterized by abuse or mistreatment even when safer and more secure options are available to us.

We may meet up with healthy candidates for relationship but consider them boring or uninteresting.

Putting up with pain is a form of giving up on our own strength, a loss of self-trust. Here are some possible reasons that people stay put in relationships that hurt rather than move on to greener pastures—or at least safer pastures. They apply to any stuckness in life or any failure to launch. Notice that most of them are examples of despair.

- To go requires letting go. That means grieving the failure or abuse, something we resist.
- Most painful situations become so gradually, and we become used to them. Our suffering becomes an absorption in a drama rather than a pointer to the exit. We may be like the frog in water that is being heated gradually. It is less likely to hop out quickly, as it would if it were thrown into water already boiling.
- The painful circumstances may be *familiar* in both senses: they resemble our family background, and we feel accustomed to them. They have become so routine that we fail to notice that they are unacceptable. There is a natural link between familiarity and safety. Unless we break that connection, we are at the mercy of it. The real safety is in our daring to move on, not in our standing still, waiting for a push.
- "The devil you know is better than the devil you don't know" may be the superstition we live by, a fear of the unknown.
- "Nothing better will come along" is an attitude that reflects an inability to imagine an alternative, which is itself another form of despair.
- Inertia may be happening: a body at rest tends to stay that way, a default setting that can lead to sloth.
- Some of us were brought up to believe that the purpose of life is to endure pain rather than to be happy. Then put-

ting up with a predicament of ongoing abuse can seem like fulfilling our main life purpose. Our religion may promise a reward in the hereafter if we endure pain now. This confirms our despondency about deserving happiness today.

- Connection of any kind may be more important than happiness.
- Intervals of happiness—intermittent reinforcement—make us more likely to stay put.
- We may convince ourselves: "It's not that bad" or "not that bad yet."
- Physical acute pain yields to healing so we associate pain with a positive result.
- We may believe that this is the only relationship possible for us since we are so inadequate—our fate.
- We may believe that our suffering will attract a rescuer to save us, so our best bet is to make sure our victimization is dramatic, obvious, and enduring.
- We might believe that we can rescue the one who brings pain into our life. Moving into the rescuer archetype raises our pain threshold. We then become obsessed with helping a partner who wants to continue his or her dysfunctional behavior. Our partner's story becomes our own. This is an inappropriate loyalty that interferes with our going on in our own life.
- We engage in wishful thinking that things will change for the better. Such false hope is a form of despair, since we have given up on our own power and insight. Real hope is based on actual evidence of progress.
- We may be hesitant "for fear to be a king," as Emily Dickinson wrote, afraid of the blossoming of our own powers, which happens when we take a courageous step out of pain.
- Someone may be telling us not to make a move, and we are following orders. Then our obedience, not an adult

virtue except for the orderly running of society, becomes
our obstacle to getting on with our own life.

- We might be waiting our turn to hurt the other person.
Our stubborn desire to take suitable revenge or to prove
something to ourselves or others can hold us back tragically and pathetically.

- We may be so dependent on or attached to the material
goods that have resulted from a relationship that we might
stay in it so as not to lose them.

- Moving out of our unpleasant lifestyle means we have
chosen to move on to the next chapter of life. We might
unconsciously be afraid that thereby we are one era closer
to our death. So our remaining on the stage of agony now
is our way of avoiding the final curtain. *Are we such subtle
escapists?*

Our personal history shows that sometimes our expectations
have been magnificently met. At other times, we have been let
down. Yet something in us keeps trying nonetheless to trust
again. We keep placing our tender trust in hearts that may turn
out, this time, to be warm flesh, not cold stone. That quality is
the essence of optimism, something to be proud of. When it
becomes a long-term style, however, it is the codependency
that makes us servile to those who hurt us. Then we have "trust
entrenched in narrow pain," as Emily Dickinson describes it.
We are codependent when we *stay* where we are hurt, deceived,
or disappointed over and over. Some of us deny the evidence
for untrustworthiness in the hope that real love and commitment might develop later, and we are willing to wait. Such
waiting is the opposite of getting on with life. We keep waiting
for more where there is only the same or even less.

One way to move out of codependency is to update what

may have been an unhealthy childhood definition of love, as we have, for instance, updated our definition of a suitable diet. If showing love included people-pleasing, putting up with abuse, and not speaking up or showing authentic feelings, our definition is harming us. The adult meaning of showing love is an attitude of loving-kindness toward others while maintaining healthy love of ourselves through self-care, stating boundaries, refusing to tolerate abuse, and being honest about our feelings.

When the way we show love toward others now is based on a self-defeating definition, we are putting ourselves at risk in many ways: People-pleasing drains our creativity. Continual abuse wrecks our self-esteem. Not speaking up can make us doubt ourselves. Holding back on our feelings reduces and depletes our lively energy.

Our years in an empty, deadlocked marriage with no intimacy, no sex, no sense of being deeply loved, are not reckoned only in time. They are shovelfuls of sand that relentlessly bury us. Moreover, the full extent of the deleterious impact—the diminishment of our spirit—can elude us. We may never even realize how cunningly and unalterably our hearts are being narrowed and mangled by staying in such a cheerless relationship—just as we may never know how insidiously pollution is affecting our bodies. We can't escape the air, but we can escape the house, if only we can wrest the key from the hand of fear.

If we finally do leave a situation that has become empty, abusive, or untrustworthy, we may wonder whether we are being vindictive. It helps to distinguish two motivations for leaving: To "take my marbles and go" in order to get back at someone is retaliation. To leave what cannot work so we can find self-healing, with no intention to hurt the other, is not retaliation but the maintaining of healthy boundaries and a choice for happiness, the choice we all deserve.

The only thing we have to fear is fear itself—nameless,
unreasoning, unjustified terror which paralyzes needed
efforts to convert retreat into advance.

—FRANKLIN DELANO ROOSEVELT,

FIRST INAUGURAL ADDRESS, 1933

Practices for Rebuilding Broken Trust

We know that our trust in our partner is based on a record of his or her trustworthiness. When there has been a breakdown of trust, the record no longer stands. If our partner wants to save the relationship and is willing to give up the infidelity and work on restoration of the commitment, rebuilding trust is risky because now all we have to go on is a promise, not a record. And that promise is from someone who has just betrayed us. We are entering an in-between space in which all we can do is risk trusting until a new record of trustworthiness is established. It is up to us to decide whether salvaging the relationship is worth taking that chance. If it is, the following practices will help.

NOTICING HOW OUR PAST IS PRESENT

Rebuilding trust is a practice that does not apply only to a relationship in which the trust has been broken. Most of us are rebuilding trust all our lives because of early or later abuse, neglect, abandonments, and disappointments. Broken trust in our present relationship triggers similar issues from childhood or past relationships, so when trust breaks down in the present, we are most ripe for the work of tackling and healing the past. We know our old griefs are being resolved when our grievances are gone.

A helpful practice is distinguishing our *experiencing self* from our *observing self.* The experiencing self is the part of us that is immersed in our feelings and thoughts. The observing self is the part of us that can more dispassionately witness our experience—it's our larger awareness and wisdom. For example, the experiencing self says, "I feel threatened. The people I love always leave me." The observing self, a more objective witness, says, "This betrayal is triggering a memory from the past. Since this is more about the past than the present, I am being invited to work on my unfinished business."

This practice is not about choosing the observer over the experiencer. It's not an either-or. Noticing and accepting *both as real* is the wisdom that supports our healing and growth. To deny or ridicule the experiencing self decreases self-trust and shames us. This practice works best when we can identify with both selves simultaneously: "I feel this *and* I realize it is a trigger reaction from the past *and* I still feel this." Then a coherent narrative can follow, and we can address, process, and resolve our past, yet still present, fear. This is how we gain a perspective that is not fear-driven.

Here is what the practice may sound like:

I feel hurt and scared as I see my life falling apart because of my partner's infidelity.

This combination of hurt and fear is familiar—which does not lessen the wallop of this recent event.

I let myself remember my story from both childhood and adult relationships. This is how I simultaneously *address* what is happening now and what happened in the past.

I let myself feel my hurt as sadness. I let myself feel my fear fully with no attempt to escape from it. I let myself feel my anger toward all the people in my life who have betrayed me. This is how I *process* what went before and connect it to what is going on now.

I notice I am *resolving* some of my unfinished emotional business by practicing this as much as is necessary. I keep focusing on my story and my work, not on revenge against my partner.

Now I realize that my fear is a throwback to a time in my life when I was powerless. My commitment to this practice is restoring my powers.

My affirmations are: I allow all my feelings and am free of fear. I am using this event as an opportunity to heal my past and increase my adult powers.

A caveat is necessary: Our intellectual knowledge of our past is always a representation of it, not necessarily what actually happened. We presume that our thinking gives us an accurate portrayal of reality, but it may simply be reflecting itself, like an image of ourselves in a mirror. In any case, we can work with our memories and find the most accurate version of them. This can happen when our cellular, bodily, feelings and sensations evoke our implicit memory of what happened to us in the past: "I lose my power when someone shows anger toward me." We join this to an explicit memory narrative: "My father used to hit me, and I could not hit back." The early experience of anger was associated with powerlessness. We know a reaction is from childhood when it is strong and we are not.

When we recognize this connection, bodily memory becomes personal history. We can work with it by acknowledging that fact and feeling our feelings as indicators of our present *strength to move on*. Then we are no longer victims of what happened to us long ago. We are victims when the memories remain unconscious. We are victims when the old connections seem real and become hooks and triggers that initiate a dysfunctional reaction. This practice can release us from such conditioning.

THE WORK OF THE PARTNER WHO BROKE TRUST

If you are the unfaithful partner, whether you want to leave the relationship or stay in it, this part of the practice is the same:

Admit what you did, honestly and fully, to your partner.

Show your sorrow about the pain your partner has been feeling, including compassion for her pain and acceptance of her anger, without defending your position.

Make the amends that you and your partner agree upon.

Stay with your partner as you both work through the restructuring or ending of your relationship.

If you plan to stay in the relationship, you can also:

Commit to end this infidelity and to remain monogamous for the future.

Focus on rebuilding trust in the relationship, using therapy if necessary, and work with the practice below, entitled "When Both Partners Want to Work on the Relationship."

If the issue is not limited to this instance of infidelity but is part of a sex addiction, join a twelve-step program. To demand that a partner trust us when we refuse recovery is saying, "Join me in my denial."

Finally, pay special attention to what is missing in yourself. Earlier in this chapter, we explored how our infidelity points to "what is missing in our relationship." This usually refers to a lack in our partner. We then look for or come upon someone who can give us what our partner lacks. However, "what is missing" also refers to something awry in the inner life of the partner who is having the affair.

The fact that any affair has an addictive, compulsive quality is a clue that we are trying to fill a need inside that may be a bottomless pit, an indicator that it is an unmet need from our childhood. *Thus, the issue for us when we are unfaithful is not only what is missing in our relationship but what is overly needed by us.*

Generally, when a need was met in a healthy way in early life, we have the capacity to be satisfied with a moderate amount of that need fulfillment ever after. However, our unmet needs have an altogether different fate. They become insatiable. This, as we saw above, leads to an addictive clinging to and obsession with anyone who seems to offer just the brand of fulfillment we always wanted. The excitement and sense of appreciation we feel toward the one who makes this happen makes us feel that we are in love. In authentic love, repose follows union. Insatiability is a signal that we are mistaking immediate fulfillment for full-on love.

The work is to mourn our past with all its unmet needs and to acknowledge with an unconditional yes just how inadequate our childhood was.*

When we do this without blame or hate toward our parents, we begin to free ourselves from our past. Our *search* for someone who can give us all we missed becomes an *openness* to the manifold ways it can happen—for example, through friends, career accomplishments, self-esteem, the sense of being held by a higher power.

Our validation then comes from within. We learn to hold our need without going outside our relationship and without

---

* I explore all this in detail and present practices that can serve as resources in my book *When the Past Is Present: Healing the Emotional Wounds That Sabotage Our Relationships* (Shambhala, 2008).

putting too much pressure on our primary relationship to get it met. As a result, we notice a natural toning down of our need, something we can't discipline ourselves into. It happens as a consequence of our work on ourselves. Without that work, we are sitting ducks for the next person who comes along and winks at us in just that special way.

THE PERSONAL WORK OF THE PARTNER WHO WAS BETRAYED

Mourning is our practice when we experience a loss of trust. We let ourselves feel sadness that our trust is lost, anger at the one taking it away, and fear that we will never find it again. We stay with the feelings of grief for as long as they are up for us. This automatically leads to a letting go of our pain, and we stop blaming ourselves or anyone else.

It is important to pay particular attention to our anger, defined as displeasure at an injustice. This means that anger is appropriate when it is based on the breaking of an agreement, a hurt at the heart level. Alternatively, an expectation is held by only one person. We are hurt at the ego level because our sense of entitlement was not honored. That anger is a frustration that can become aggressive and unhealthy. When we are committed to personal integrity, we look within ourselves to explore our anger. If it is appropriate, based on the breaking of a bilateral agreement, we express our anger directly to our partner, always nonviolently. When our anger is the indignation of our disappointed ego, we call ourselves on our projections and expectations. Then we bring our whole experience—and our unsatisfactory partner—to our loving-kindness practice.

In either case, we eventually find healing for ourselves when we come to see the infidelity as a fact. We say yes to the reality without further protest. This attitude of unconditional yes moves us in the direction of full acceptance of what happened to our relationship and puts us in the best position to deal with it. We do not condone what happened. We do not become involved in the drama that happened between our partner and his lover. To the extent we can stay focused on ourselves and what is up next for our own relationship with our partner, we are in the best position for healing.

All this applies only to a single affair or instance of infidelity. If infidelities keep happening or are part of a general and ongoing rejection of intimacy, we do not have the makings of a healthy relationship and need to confront that, probably most appropriately in therapy.

If the infidelity is a form of revenge, hate, or meanness toward us, then therapy is not sufficient. This level of malice requires a spiritual conversion to loving-kindness if there is ever to be repentance and true amendment.

If the betrayed partner has steered the other into an affair, for whatever reason, the issue requires careful inquiry into what the relationship is really about and what resentments or despair are in the mix.

If our partner's infidelity is part of a sex addiction, our practice is to join a twelve-step program such as S-Anon.

In any case, commitments like these can help:

I let go of my pictures of who I thought you were.
I let go of any demand that you live up to them.
I will not retaliate.
I look for ways to forgive but to maintain my boundaries too. (When we forgive, we let go of our attachment to the one whose offenses have occupied us. Thus, forgiveness represents a healthy separation, a maintaining of bound-

aries, a freedom from attachment. *We also let go of blame and the need to get back at the person who offended us.* Forgiveness thereby gives us the opportunity to reconnect and the freedom to move on.)
I send loving-kindness to you every day and to myself too.
I move along on my own journey.
I move along on the journey we are on together, if that can happen. Then, I offer to begin again with you by addressing, processing, resolving our issues.

We know we are becoming healthier and more spiritually aware when our focus is less and less on how the other hurt us. We orient ourselves instead toward three concerns: how we can gain in wisdom from our experience, how the betrayal has become an opportunity to practice mindfulness and loving-kindness, and where we go from here.

As long as we are demanding absolute trust from anyone or anything—no hurts, no broken promises, no letdowns—we are backing out of the most touching, vitalizing, and soul-deepening chapters of the human chronicle.

WHEN BOTH PARTNERS WANT TO WORK ON THE RELATIONSHIP

If both partners want to stay together and rebuild trust, the program is to explore the relationship and the infidelity, usually in the context of therapy.

This means looking into our trust histories, our fears of commitment, our sex life, our resentments and appreciations, our willingness and reluctance to start over. We focus on addressing our needs, calling them by name, admitting how long we have been unsatisfied. Then we process the infidelity by showing our feelings and noticing how they are connected to issues in our past. This leads to agreements about changing our relationship radically. These agreements can begin with the commitments listed at the end of the practice entitled "The Personal Work of the Partner Who Was Betrayed."

In addition, we can make commitments such as these to each other:

> I commit myself to trust you and to be trustworthy toward you.
> I will respect your boundaries.
> I will be honest about my feelings and behavior.
> I will be open to your needs and share mine with you.
> No matter what you do from here on in, I will never retaliate, though I will say "Ouch!" while looking for healthy ways to work things out with you.
> When a problem arises, I want to listen to your concerns and join you in addressing, processing, and resolving our issue.
> If our problems become too big for us to handle on our own, I am very willing to go to therapy.
> My main commitment is to remain loyal and present to you. I plan to do this in any way I can and definitely by these five A's:

> Paying *attention* to you and your feelings.
> *Accepting* you as you are.
> *Appreciating* you and stating it often.
> Showing you *affection* in physical ways without having it be sexual every time.
> *Allowing* you the freedom to live in accord with your own deepest needs, values, and wishes while trusting you to remain faithful to our life as a couple.

The challenge is to form a new mutual understanding that commits both partners to a continual exchange of the five A's and unconditional honesty. This includes keeping each other abreast of feelings, doubts, and agendas. It is an uphill struggle to rebuild trust, the equivalent of starting a relationship over. But it can be done as long as both partners are willing to do the work and keep doing it for as long as it takes to restabilize the relationship or place it on a new footing.

In addition to therapy, trust also builds in a relationship when the partners do things together that involve them in having an experience that is outside their home but that they engage in side by side—for example, going camping or skiing together, going on a retreat. A weekend together each month certainly increases intimacy.

Especially useful is mutual engagement in active lifestyle sports, events, or projects that require careful concentration so that both partners have their attention drawn to something that takes them out of themselves fully. Building such mutually enjoyable and outward-focused experiences into any life together is a fast track to becoming closer as a couple.

Consider also your motivation for rebuilding: do you want to reestablish your relationship because it means a lot to you? A way of knowing the answer to this question is to ask why you want to be with each other. If the answer is "Because we have children, are compatible, have a history, or have nowhere else to go," your motivation is not enthusiastic enough to make for a real change.

If your answer is "Because we still love each other immensely, are really into each other, and are ready to make a full commitment to each other," your motivation gives hope that the relationship can indeed come back to life.

In the first instance, you are settling for low stakes, adapting, reconciling yourself to the original status quo, seeking safety and security. In the second instance, you are animated by a chance at having the relationship you always wanted with the person you are really excited to be with.

You may notice that your way of relating in the recent past has been uncommitted, lackluster, or on-again, off-again. After an affair, both of you may realize that you cannot go back to the way it was. Half-in, half-out does not seem to be an option anymore. The opportunity opening to you is for total commitment to make the relationship all it can be with every agreement cheerfully kept, no holds barred and no hold-outs. Anything less will surely feel insincere, inadequate, and unfair to both of you.

There are indeed only two choices now: an unconditional commitment so you can take hold and move on together or a breakup so you can let go and move on separately. Both choices represent healthy change because both eventually lead you to your own truth. That means so much more than half-measures that avail nothing. I am reminded of an Italian saying: "meglio soli che mal accompagnati," which means "better alone than badly joined." From the half position we maintain the status quo and go nowhere. From the nothing position, we can go anywhere.

As we have been seeing, when it comes to rebuilding trust, any couple coming out of an episode of infidelity has a strike against it: it takes a while for the betrayed person to trust her partner and for the betrayer to establish a record of trustworthiness. Neither one can be expected to be enthusiastic for some time. Rather, you can expect to be tense and angry and to have low interest in each other for a while. This is not the best position from which to do the work, so patience becomes part of the commitment.

The mourning referred to in these practices is not only for

the breakdown of trust. It is also for the low ebb your relationship had fallen to before the infidelity. It is also for your mutual willingness to tolerate that situation for as long as you did. This more extensive realization of where the unhingements and losses have been helps move the rebuilding process along. It is a delicate operation in any case, but it can be done.

All the mysterious angles in the infidelity issue make it larger than any list of practices can exhaust. The four practices above are like steps A, B, C, and D, and the rest of the alphabet awaits attention from each of us in his or her own way and time. This is because any seriously wounding betrayal or deception leads to a grief that does not yield to griefwork, no matter how long we engage in it.

Our more exacting, elusive, and subtle practice is to grow beyond the betrayal. We do this when a breakdown in trust is seen as a call to evolve beyond blindly trusting the promises humans make and beyond hating those who break them. Then we become bigger than our story. Our life is Buddha-size, not ego-size anymore.

For women, betrayal hits hard because the female psyche is so much about relatedness: "We had something special between us, and you gave it away to a stranger," or "I wanted something special, and you did not give it to me but did give it to someone else." For men, an infidelity may hit at the ego level: "I thought you were mine, and what was mine went elsewhere." Both possibilities can, of course, apply to either sex.

In addition, for any of us, trust has a spiritual dimension, so the betrayal is a loss at that level too. That territory is not reclaimed through strategies but by the grace of time and the practices of mindfulness and loving-kindness.

Finally, we do well to acknowledge that not everything that

has been broken can be mended. A naive belief within the self-help movement is that any problem within a relationship can be processed and resolved, given enough effort and therapy. That is not always the case, as our life experience has sometimes shown. Sadly, some events that happen in a partnership remain irresolvable, so all we can do is let go of our relationship and move on along our own path. This is, understandably, a daunting challenge for us. To let go of a relationship is to let go of all the encouraging hope that it might have worked. To go on is to be alone, a most unwelcome prospect. After all, we are the beings whose history began with the importance of huddling together and who have evolved to the importance of cuddling together.

The fact that not everything can be mended—or ended—also has a positive dimension. The element of inconsolability in major griefs, the way some regrets hang on, the stamina of certain memories, may all be serving us quite well. Perhaps the lasting impact of inexpugnable griefs is silently making us more sensitive, more creative, more compassionate, more humble.

Our hearts hold such labyrinthine ways, who knows how they really work? Maybe they can open fully only through hurt. Maybe their most profound beat is the echo of an ache.

Recently, I tried to throw away a seemingly useless program in my computer. A message popped up: "This item cannot be eliminated because it is required to make your system work effectively." We can trust that our psyche operates in that same way. Some events and feelings remain raggedly unsettled in us, and we have to trust that they make our human system work better—who knows how? This may explain why not every one of our psychological issues can, or is meant to, be fully addressed, finally processed, or completely resolved.

Our assignment is only to let go of our relentless need to control our feelings and to keep granting hospitality to our story, with all its gaps in need of mending and all its griefs that have no tidy ending.

What a complex and enigmatic challenge it is to understand—and to become—fully human.

> *It takes just such evil and painful things for the great emancipation to occur.*
>
> —Friedrich Nietzsche, *Beyond Good and Evil*

6

Trusting Ourselves

IN MANY ANCIENT TRIBAL RITUALS, a vision quest moves a young man from the comforts of his familiar surroundings to challenges in an unknown zone. Survival in this venture helps the initiate trust himself. His trust extends also to the transcendent forces that succor him as assisting guides. He can trust their accompaniment, internally and externally, in all he does from then on.

In our civilized culture, there are very few rituals like that, with the exception of wilderness experiences and some others. Most of us have to learn to trust ourselves by hook or by crook. We have no specific path outlined for us by society. Most of us learn to trust ourselves proportionally to how adept and nimble we can become as we face our predicaments. The skills are a combination of what we have learned willy-nilly and from how firmly we pull on our own bootstraps.

Trusting ourselves happens when we are generally happy

about who we have become, able to love others in a committed way, engaged in meaningful work, not under the sway of addictions, and capable of handling daily stresses. Trust in ourselves will therefore manifest itself as equanimity, going with the flow.

Here are some specific qualities of healthy self-trust that simultaneously provide a profile of psychological health:

We have a sense of autonomy and act responsibly.

We perceive reality more and more as it is rather than through fantasies, projections, and transferences.

We are not directed by our past but live in the present with an intention geared toward a future of appropriate goals.

We have a support system and are part of others' support systems.

We give and receive the five A's—attention, acceptance, appreciation, affection, and allowing—in relationships.

We give the five A's to ourselves.

In times of stress, we have the ability to self-soothe and look for strength within rather than escape into self-destructive behavior or inappropriate dependency on others.

We are not overwhelmed by changes in our intimate relationship nor scared off by an opportunity for intimacy to deepen.

We can adjust to comings and goings without being overwhelmed by a sense of engulfment or abandonment.

We are comfortable with our own feelings and with those of others, expressing them when it is safe to do so and not expressing them when it is unsafe.

We come to terms with fear and guilt so that they neither hamper nor drive our behavior and choices.

We face disappointment and frustration without becoming destabilized.

We are animated by a zest for life, playfulness, and a sense of humor.

We act assertively but not aggressively.

We can set reasonable boundaries on how much we will give or on how far others can go in their demands upon us.

Our style in life and in relationship is to be open rather than to coerce, to prompt rather than to poke.

We have the ability to put off immediate gratification when necessary.

We act with integrity and live in accord with life-affirming values, such as generosity, truthfulness, and respect toward everyone regardless of their status or their attitude toward us.

We are working on our ego so that we are not compelled by fear of not looking good, attachment to being right, arrogance, control, or entitlement.

We realize that we have a shadow side and are willing to explore it, especially when it shows up in our behavior. Entitlement is the shadow side of trust. The shadow side of trustworthiness is being loyal when it no longer serves either party.

We let go of any relationship or system that endorses self-negation or discourages critical thinking.

We see our lives as having a purpose and meaning that align with the evolution of the planet, and we are committed to growing in consciousness of that universal destiny and making our unprecedented contribution in accord with our unique gifts and talents.

A relationship that supports all this helps trust to flourish. Our true self has been waiting for its cue to make a personal appearance. That cue is the five A's given to us by ourselves and by those who love us.

In his book *I and Thou,* Martin Buber commented on how our need for one another is directly related to our ability to trust ourselves: "A person wishes to be confirmed in his being by another person. . . . Secretly and bashfully, he watches for a Yes which allows him to be and which can come only from one human person to another. It is from one human being to another that the heavenly bread of self-being is passed." Thus, self-trust is not a cancellation of our need for others, only a recognition that they can help us enormously by confirming us in the pleasure of being ourselves.

Many of us were brought up by parents who did not focus on helping us *launch* ourselves in the world as powerful independent beings who loved being ourselves. Instead, they may have focused on keeping us *attached* to them. We trust ourselves now when we self-launch and maintain bonds with others at the same time. No relationship can stop us from launching ourselves into who we really are and into achieving what we want. Likewise, no launch eliminates the need for bonds with others.

Our default setting is sometimes inertia, the opposite of launching. We learn to trust ourselves when we act despite our inertia and take the steps that move us along on our journey. Part of this is acknowledging that our inertia today cannot be pinned on our parents. Our parents' behavior in our past does not make the case for staying in our stuckness now. We can trust that to be our own choice by this time.

We learn to trust our choices by launching ourselves into actions that reflect what we really are and want. Most of us have an image of what we are supposed to be like, especially as men or women. This set of do's and don'ts can be a barrier to the full release of our authentic needs and wishes.

We men may not be able to tolerate or even contemplate anything incompatible with "the male image." For example, Malcolm is married happily, but he cannot deny that he occasionally wants to dress in women's clothes, a familiar desire since childhood. He can allow himself to be curious, visiting Internet sites that specialize in images of cross-dressers. If Malcolm does try on women's clothes, he may feel regret or even disgust later. This is his way of canceling the desire and feeling "normal" again. Malcolm cannot simply "go for it" and do what he wants to do because of the incompatibility of his fantasy with the demands of his male persona. Malcolm is not a free man. But freedom is less valuable to him than maintaining the image of being the man society has decreed. His self-image is not wide enough to accommodate the full spectrum of who he is—or of what humanity can include.

We truly trust ourselves only when *nothing about us is incompatible anymore except doing harm to ourselves or others.* Then this line by the ancient Roman poet dramatist Terence becomes our motto: "Nothing human is alien to me."

Trusting Our Feelings

Strong feelings in our childhood household might have been the preamble to abuse or out-of-control behavior. Now intense feelings toward us by other adults may trigger an expectation that the same results will follow. This may be part of why we fear (do not trust) feelings in ourselves and others.

We may not trust our tears, fearing we may never stop crying. We may not trust our anger, fearing we may become aggressive and hurt someone. Most of us fear going directly into our feelings, yet this is how we learn to trust them and thereby trust ourselves. It is certainly an adult task to supervise our feelings so we can express them appropriately. But we go too far when we shut them down altogether. When we stifle our sobs, we lose a skillful means to trust ourselves.

As we trust ourselves more, we also let go of our fear of our own physical impulses and allow unguarded, nonplanned moments. We fire the internal referee who scrutinizes our every move, and we trust ourselves on any playing field. We know we may fumble, but we will stay in the game. In our psychological work and spiritual practices, we do not feel regret if we do not win the day by our efforts. Vietnamese Buddhist teacher Thich Nhat Hanh is a model of this when he reports that he and his fellow Buddhists eventually realized that they could not achieve victory through the antiwar movement in Vietnam, but, nonetheless, he has never regretted the protests he participated in back then. At least he was spreading compassion and affirming a commitment to ending the violence in his country. If occasionally he still feels some tug of regret, he can simply hold it rather than be chained by it. We too can do that with our regrets.

We can act with dedication and unceasing effort but with no claim upon or attachment to an outcome. We can free ourselves from demanding that our preferences be honored—such as the preference for pleasure, not pain; gain, not loss; fame, not shame; praise, not blame—though we may still wish for them. Instead, we do all within our means so the best can happen, then let the chips fall where they may and make the best of where they fell.

Our most rudimentary feelings are sadness, anger, fear, and exuberance. The acronym *SAFE* fits these feelings, since we gained the capacity to feel our feelings in an uninhibited way when we felt *safe* to do so in childhood. Safety engenders trust. If that did not happen, we can learn to feel freely and safely from other adults in our present life who encourage and confirm us in what we feel. As we see others trusting our feelings, we trust them too. It is never too late to show our feelings.

When we repress our feelings, they are stored in our body and enacted indirectly in our behavior. When we allow our feelings to emerge rather than cover them up, deny them, or evade them, they become friendly—that is, constructive and positive. This is because we are achieving equanimity, an ever-increasing comfort with all that occurs and an evenness in our feelings. We experience this as self-trust, since we are trusting that we will express our feelings without aggression toward others and the feelings will appropriately fit our circumstances.

> If we lose, we will be *sad,* but we will not collapse into an unending grief. We grieve first, then find equanimity, not the other way around. Only after our feelings are felt and expressed can our equanimity be real. Otherwise, it is stoicism, an indifference about what happens in order to avoid appropriate feelings.
>
> If we are *angry,* we will show it nonviolently. We will not use our anger in an aggressive or violating way. We will not turn it inward to protect others from our legitimate feeling. We now trust that the legitimacy of any feeling comes from having it.
>
> If we are threatened, we will feel *fear,* but we will not let the fear stop us from taking action to protect ourselves. We accept that fear will always be in us; we have no control over that. But we do not have to let it stop or drive us ever again.
>
> If good things happen, we can release ourselves into *exuberance* without using drugs or alcohol as our way of celebrating.

We might also say, "I can't control my feelings, but I don't have to judge myself for them. I don't have to be possessed by them. I don't have to let them take up long-term residence, nor do I have to evict them. All that is required is that I greet their arrival with hospitality and watch them leave with composure."

Mindfulness moves us in that direction because it means just such presence in the here and now. A fundamental feature of trusting ourselves is our confidence that we have it in us to understand and handle our feelings and urges. Ignorance is believing that we are inadequate, the equivalent of no longer trusting our own inner wholeness.

When we are free of ego chatter, sitting in mindful silence, a field of awareness opens that feels immensely trustworthy. The more we trust our awareness, the more do we trust our inner voice, the wise inner witness—always a breath away—as a source of safety and security. Shakespeare wrote in *Measure for Measure:*

> Go to your bosom;
> Knock there, and ask your heart what it
> doth know. . . .

In that heart space, we have ourselves as the safe base to come back to. This eliminates the need for the usual buttresses and bulwarks meant to keep us away from our feelings. We can be defense-less at last, with an openness, a yes to what is, and a lively responsiveness. This trust in our own inherent sanity and wisdom is our personal realization of safety.

We begin to see the power of deep mindfulness with regard to feelings. We trust our feelings when we no longer have to manage our anxiety in healthy or unhealthy ways. With long practice of mindfulness, our feelings can come through with a clarity that requires no further action or closure on our part, not even addressing, processing, resolving. Deep practice of mindfulness can integrate some experiences all by itself. This is because we are not trying to defend our identity, only to open. Then every feeling and event is no longer an inquiry into who we are and how to process our experience but an exploration of how we can sit, how we can stay present in the midst of whatever happens. *Now our interest is not in what happened but in how to stay with what happens.*

When we no longer have to figure something out, strategize about it, or fix it, we know what it really means to be here now. From this position of mindful presence, of unconditional allowing, we can relate to others freely because our ego is no longer standing in the way. The title of this book says it: when we dare to trust ourselves, we open to real love and intimacy.

LEAR: *You see how this world goes.*
GLOUCESTER: *I see it feelingly.*
—SHAKESPEARE, *KING LEAR*

Practice

WORKING WITH OUR EMOTIONS

In the style of mindfulness, emotions—no matter how upsetting, daunting, or dramatic—are simply felt and let go of. We simultaneously let go of the story attached to our feelings. We need both of these to restructure our conscious life—showing our feelings while letting go of our story lines. Paradoxically, we can also notice our story lines long enough to see through them.

For instance, perhaps we are sad about how someone was disloyal to us. We feel the feeling with all our ego mind-sets and story lines turned on full blast. This includes obsession with the meaning, origin, and goal of our experience as well as judgment, blame, fantasy, comparison, shame, and how they story-tell us about our inadequacies or victimizations.

We notice the stress in this, but we also notice we can survive it because we are no longer compelled to act on it. This leads to a sense of power *in* our emotions. We then allow ourselves equal time to sit and feel the feeling purely without the inhibitions that come from ego mindsets. This mindful style leads to an empowering equanimity. We continue back and forth between the two styles, serene mindfulness and dramatic mind-sets. But, with each go-around, we commit ourselves to increase our time in the mindful style. As we gradually cease engaging so much in the dramatic style, *our serenity becomes more important and more interesting than our story.* We have diminished its authority.

Both ingredients are necessary as we restructure how we experience feelings, thoughts, and events. We restructure our conscious life when we feel our feelings *and* notice our editorial comments without having to take orders from them anymore.

Thus, my mind-sets —my judgments, story-lines, and defenses— are tamed into spiritual consciousness:

In mindfulness I pause long enough to find a path between my stories and mind-sets. In that gap I access a wisdom and sanity not available to me in the heat of my ego theatrics.

Then I let my feelings emerge nakedly, free of the costumes designed by my story and my ego expectations.

As my feelings play themselves out fully, but without compulsion or aggression, only serenity and loving-kindness remain.

I find the equanimity to let people and things be as they are with no further need to avoid or control them.

I now welcome what happens to me with lively responsiveness. I can feel myself thereby dismantling my futile, long-entrenched tendency to keep things running smoothly so that my emotions never burst open.

I am realizing that sanity and enlightenment have always been within me and I have been granted this lifetime to uncover them.

Our life begins with a need for reliability so we can learn to trust. Our life matures when we learn to live with uncertainty. To live between such bookends makes our journey marvelously intriguing.

Trusting Our Bodies

Mr. Duffy lived at a little distance from his body.
—JAMES JOYCE, *DUBLINERS,* "A PAINFUL CASE"

Our body is a field of experience. As we pay attention to it, we are in the best position to learn from it. We may notice that it is constricted or tightened and tense in some ways. Yet we can use our body for deep breaths and other physical techniques that help release our tension. Our body is thus both a signal system and a resource system. Our body is a reliable teaching, what in Buddhism is called an unsurpassed, penetrating, and perfect dharma.

The more aware we are of our own bodies, the more alert we are to other people and the more empathic we become, because we read their emotional states more intuitively and accurately. In that way, our bodies also help us to love.

Thoughts seem more authoritative to us than bodily sensations, but that is a prejudice. Once we let go of granting so much clout to our thinking, we can more easily let our body become a tool of listening. We will know how to relax: we will remember to breathe consciously, to take a hot bath on stressful days, or to make time for good, clean fun. Play encourages our brain centers of relaxation to kick in. Success at calming our mind and soothing our body leads to self-regulation and balance. This is an ability that helps us trust ourselves.

We harm our bodies and render them numb when we over-work and exhaust ourselves. When our work is our true call-ing, it does not tire us but animates us. That is not always possible, so our challenge becomes alternating stressful work with play, an alternative energy source. The less appealing our job, the more are we committed to using our leisure for re-newal, enjoyment, and relaxation.

In cortisol-drenched trauma, it is well-nigh impossible for most of us to relax or meditate, even with the help of deep breaths or hot baths. Our perturbation may seem to us to be only mental. Yet it is in our bodies even more fiercely in the form of a speedy heartbeat, shallow breathing, trembling, tightness in the stomach or throat, higher blood pressure, cold sweat, and so on.

Likewise, trauma from our past is encoded in our cells with no story, only feeling. This may be because the hippocampus, the area of the brain that stores explicit memories, can be com-promised by stress. Thus, present trauma feels the same as that from early life when we were powerless to fight it.

Our body generally reports our gross needs to us, not the sub-tle versions of them. We must therefore be careful about taking any of our needs literally. They are metaphors. Thus, a need for sex may mean a need for holding. A strong desire for doughnuts may really indicate the need to fill a sense of emptiness.

We may also feel anxious when it seems more appropriate to feel excited. For instance, looking forward to a first date or to a sexual encounter may evoke apprehension. The coin of adrenaline has two sides, anxiety and excitement. When our anxiety does not soon turn into excitement, the message is: "Be-ware. This plan, date, or person may not fit for you." An abuse or distress may be triggered from our past. Our anxiety may also flow from habit and not be a warning at all. Our body tells our story but it is often hard to decode. Competent bodywork and somatic therapy help us translate.

Some of our needs are hidden even from ourselves. For instance, if it was dangerous to be close to a parent because he used that as a pretext for abusing us, we might not even be able to know that we need closeness now. Likewise, when our needs led to feeling shamed or threatened, we may now be hiding them, even from ourselves.

Finally, we notice that our bodies can grant us a physically felt sense of our coherence and continuity. Here is an example from my own life. I decided to put a pile of family photos into chronological order. I therefore laid them all out on the rug, carefully arranged them in order, then placed them into an album accordingly. When the task of turning chaos into order was finished, an unexpected thing happened to me. I had a felt sense of my place in the human story, not simply because of a historical sequence but by belonging to a family who produced me and held me throughout my lifetime—granting me a sense of my legitimacy on the planet. It was a powerful physical experience of myself as connected and therefore somehow *purposeful*. In addition, I felt a wave of kindly feeling pass through me toward all the people pictured, as I remembered them, with all their foibles and graces. A sense of contentment arose in my body, a physical sense that all that happened to me could be trusted as finally and fully satisfactory. This confirmed my belief that trust is a felt sense, not simply information. I also began to see myself as an embodied being rather than a being with a body.

> *Things are losing their hardness; even my body now lets the light through.*
>
> —Virginia Woolf, *The Waves*

Trusting Our Sexuality

Our experience of sex is another example of how influenced our bodies are by society. An inhibitive family or church may have instilled fear or shame in us about sex. That might have made us doubt the legitimacy of freely expressing—or even knowing—our unique sexuality. The original restriction keeps hurting us through the limited and constricted life we now lead. The real loss is not only that we now experience guilt or addiction in our sexual behavior. The greater harm was that the sexual part of us could not freely and fully mature because of the atmosphere of shame in our childhood. Until we have disidentified with the definitions and injunctions we inherited, we are not the authors of our own experience, not truly autonomous.

There seem to be three circuits in the brain regarding love and sex: In the testosterone/estrogen circuit is interest in sex with many people, lust with no necessity of love. In the dopamine circuit is the narrowing of focus to one person with whom we fall in love. In the oxytocin/vasopressin circuit is attachment, ongoing intimate bonding.

In the first, we are cruisers; in the second, we are possessed; in the third, we commit to staying. From nature's point of view, we cruise to find the mate who will be suitable for child producing. We fall in love to settle on the one with whom we will procreate. We remain together so the family can be secure and the children can grow accordingly. Thus, the three circuits operate to move us through three phases, usually from adolescence to mature adulthood.

The style of lust and giddily experiencing romantic love both have an addictive flavor. We become obsessed, take chances, become dependent, feel compelled to have more and more, can't let go. But this addiction does not require a program of recovery unless we become stuck in it. As long as it is a phase and time-bound, it is not harmful, unless we overdo it or extend it.

The three styles of sexuality are sequential but can also happen simultaneously. Thus, our settling into the third category does not shut down brain centers for lust or falling in love with someone else. Things get complicated when we act out those drives while in a committed relationship. But we always have the option of taking our drives and reactions as information and not acting on them. This is the discipline of fidelity.

We can, throughout the life span, learn to trust our sexual impulses and to celebrate them, without being irresponsible toward ourselves or others. Trusting our bodies sexually, for instance, means not being so caught up in an adrenaline reaction to someone that we lose our objectivity or our sanity about the choices we make.

Shakespeare, in *Antony and Cleopatra,* shows that a person to whom we are sexually tied can become a higher power:

> That kiss
> Which is my heaven to have.

Can I Trust Myself in a Crisis?

Not till we are lost . . . do we begin to find ourselves and realize where we are and the infinite extent of our relations.

—HENRY DAVID THOREAU, *WALDEN*

The landscape of the human psyche, like that of the earth, includes desert places. They are parched not by the sun, wind, and fire but by weakness, helplessness, and hopelessness. When we find ourselves in such a crisis, we can pause mindfully with no attempt to fill anything in—as a desert is an acceptable pause in the ecology. We simply contemplate the crisis and look at it without a judgment against ourselves for being in it or any compulsion to get it all fixed.

In this book, we are learning to sit as witnesses and observe the news happening now, not inventing editorials about it.

This kind of presence stabilizes us and makes it easier for us to walk through the difficult topography of our predicament. The challenge is to form a dedicated presence uninterrupted by stories or projections. Then we notice wisdom and sanity coming from and through us. This is how mindfulness contributes to our trust that we can grow in crisis. Now the practice of mindfulness has led to self-nurturance—that is, to loving-kindness toward ourselves.

In such mindful contemplation, our mind-sets need not remain operative but can be suspended. If we notice ourselves judging in the sense of censuring, we simply witness it and come back to the moment and to what we are experiencing. If we notice that we are caught in a story, we tap ourselves on the shoulder, metaphorically, and redirect our attention to what we are feeling. All of this puts us in touch with our courage, and we do not see ourselves as victims.

As we have seen, we all construct a life narrative to condemn or exculpate ourselves or others. From this story we form a fixed set of governing prejudices. They help us explain our predicaments in life and get us off the hook about truly addressing them. Mindful contemplation is a release from that sheltering avoidance. It is coming into the explicitly real rather than hiding in the implicitly illusory. We use our present crisis of helplessness to free ourselves from landing in a story. Instead, we move through our crisis into a new chapter in our lives.

The challenge is to pay attention to and stay with the here-and-now existential reality—however unsavory—while the essential truth of our inner strength and wisdom hovers in the wings ready to make a personal appearance. The paradox is in the fact that going further into hopelessness can grant access to hope. That is how contemplation is an act of trust.

When we unconditionally embrace our predicament, it becomes a threshold to something new. The "either/or" changes to "both/and." How? We do not jump into the unexplored wilderness of helplessness brandishing the banner of hope and declare it under our control. We simply stay put in our helplessness, and that fidelity creates the milieu in which real change can happen. This is possible in deep mindfulness.

In the staying put is our real trust—and hope—in ourselves. This is such a formidable issue in transitions. We have to trust our powerlessness, and that contradicts the common definition of trust as counting on someone or something's reliability! But we are in the realm of paradox, so we know that dictionary definitions do not hold. A spiritual venture is in the works, so in the context of uncertainty and powerlessness, trust is appropriate.

Powerlessness is a familiar theme in heroic journey stories. The powerlessness of the hero usually incites the archetype of assistance to appear in the form of human or divine intervention. For instance, when Pinocchio, in the 1940 Disney film, is lying waterlogged on the beach, inanimate and helpless, he attracts the attention of the heavenly Blue Fairy, who makes the brave little wooden-head into a real boy. Robin Hood is hopeless and powerless in prison, waiting to be hanged. This spurs Maid Marion to come up with a plan to save him.

Moreover, the assisting forces do not rescue the hero as they would a victim but as they would someone who is ready to stretch into his full dimensions of heroism. Thus, Robin Hood, upon release from prison, immediately continues the fight for justice. The heroes *find their own inner resources as a result of their powerlessness.* This is the real identity of the assisting force in the stories. It is not external but internal, as Luke Skywalker heard in *Star Wars:* "The force is within you." The real assisting force is being just now, just here, with just this, as just who we are.

Practices

> *Helplessness and isolation are the core experiences of psychological trauma. Empowerment and reconnection are the core experiences of recovery.*
>
> —JUDITH HERMAN, *TRAUMA AND RECOVERY*

BEFRIENDING THE THREE WITCHES

The experience of powerlessness is perceived as dangerous when we are caught in a replay of childhood or in maintaining a victim identity. Then it becomes not a transition, as in hero stories, but confusion and stuckness. That level of bewilderment and transference from the past onto the present does not attract the assisting-force archetype. It incites only self-pity and perhaps predators who seek to take advantage of our weakness. The first level of our work when transference is in the air is to acknowledge our condition, to address, process, and resolve our issues from the past with someone we trust or in therapy. Then the friend, partner, or therapist is an accompanying presence, an assisting force.

A more intriguing practice that can help us is, paradoxically, a surrendering to the three witches of weakness, helplessness, and hopelessness. We begin by recalling earlier times in life when we felt this same way, especially in childhood. We stay with these memories and then affirm that we are grown up now and have resources we did not have in the past. We choose to use the resource of surrender without being victimized by our feelings. We do this by allowing ourselves to have the full experience of weakness, helplessness, and hopelessness. We let ourselves feel them one at a time and all at once. We take deep breaths into each feeling state until we notice a softening, releasing, and relaxing. Letting go is the positive dimension of powerlessness.

By accepting our moments of helplessness as the givens of all human lives, we change the name of this feeling state from weakness to ordinary predicament. We use the resource of surrendering to that given with deep breaths and by saying the word *yes* aloud or silently with each exhale.

Then our feeling opens into new possibilities unnoticed before. We find the strength of those who let themselves have their experience regardless of whether they are certain they can handle it. The wonderful thing is that letting ourselves go into that place of helpless and unpromising discomfort is precisely what invests us with a personal power we might never have guessed was ours. The result is self-trust instead of self-loathing. We are no longer shut down, no longer down for the count. In the Twenty-third Psalm, we read, "He leads me beside the still waters; he restores my spirit." Trusting leads to that reconstituting of ourselves, arriving at a resort of serenity and a recharging of our energy.

Here is a summary of the exercise:

1. Inhabit rather than withdraw from the weakness, helplessness, and hopelessness.
2. Recall the same feeling state in earlier life.
3. Affirm that you are now mature enough to deal with it.
4. Say yes to the given that we all feel this way sometimes.
5. Stay with your feelings until a shift into serenity occurs.
6. Open to the new forms of energy that begin to appear on the horizon; take the world up on what it offers.
7. Affirm self-trust for the future: "I can always surrender to what I feel, and new energies will arise in me." This is trust in the power of the human psyche as self-restoring,

self-renewing. Yes to what is happening is the equivalent of the "He" in the psalm who "restores my spirit." That spirit is our true self.

Our practice has helped us integrate our earlier experiences so we can live in the present. Now moments of powerlessness will become not only tolerable but enormously settling. We will truly believe that they are not verdicts but valid and occasional interludes on every human path. Then:

- We notice them mindfully—that is, with no blame or shame.
- We treat ourselves with loving-kindness.
- We open ourselves to assistance.
- We recover our powers when the timing of the universe grants access. Our practice encourages the granting of that permission.

NO LONGER VICTIMS

Draw an equilateral triangle pointing downward. Write the word *victim* below the bottom angle. Write *persecutor* above the top left angle and *fighter* above the top right angle. Notice that *persecutor* and *fighter* have equal top status. The *victim* is in the one-down, powerless position. A fighter in this instance is one who stands up for herself by not letting the behavior of others, or the impact of events, victimize her. She fights and does not give up on herself. She is on a par with her persecutor. She is no longer the victim of his assaults.

Ask yourself how the angles of this triangle apply to your life now. How can you act in a way that combines self-protection with nonretaliation?

Here are eight possible ways to become a healthy ego fighter:

1. Accept the reality of your present situation as an opportunity to rise in consciousness rather than as blows to knock you down.
2. Reframe your regrets as lessons regarding how to do things in the future rather than as verdicts about how wrong you were this time.
3. Realize that regret has a healthy alternative program: mourning, making amends where necessary, and affirming a self-forgiveness. *Regret* means grieving over and over. When we do not mourn fully, our unfinished emotional business keeps revisiting us in the form of regret, an unpleasant guest.
4. See yourself working on whatever problem you are faced with from a position of strength, not as a little child with hat in hand (the style of needy dependency).
5. Say to others, "Support me" but not "Do it for me."
6. See doing all you can, rather than fully achieving a goal, as success.
7. Be willing to lose face but not to lose integrity: you may lose the goodies but not your goodness—what matters so much.
8. Let go of anything in your life now that does not support the emergence of your full powers, your authentic orientation in life, your true calling, your unabbreviated identity.

You can use the preceding list as a checklist to explore your current abilities as a healthy ego fighter and identify areas to work on.

MARK ANTONY: *Come, then; for with a wound I must be cured. . . .*

CLEOPATRA: *My desolation does begin to make*
A better life.
—SHAKESPEARE, *ANTONY AND CLEOPATRA*

A POSITIVE APPROACH TO OURSELVES

Here is a practice combining mindfulness and loving-kindness for couples or friends. One person asks, "What do you love about yourself?" The other person answers in all honesty, enumerating one after another the qualities he loves about himself, what is right with him. When he seems to run out of things to say, the other person repeats, "What do you love about yourself?" They do this until there is nothing more to add. No judgmental, shame-based, or self-effacing statements are allowed.

This is not bragging, only practicing the first part of loving-kindness—appreciating and caring about ourselves. The other person simply listens while making no comment but maintaining eye contact. This is mindful listening, free of judgment or ridicule. Then the other person takes a turn as the practice is repeated.

It will be natural for both of you to feel awkward in this exercise. That does not stop the process but gives you something to discuss after it. When we fear acknowledging our lovability, we are finding out about our ability to trust ourselves. When we fear hearing the other and maintaining eye contact, we are looking into our fears about relating on an intimate level.

We release and liberate ourselves by repeating the practice until we follow the directions, no matter how awkward this continues to feel. Then it really does work.

7

Our Core Trust in Reality

NOW WE LOOK AT CORE TRUST, the most challenging of all the directions our trust can take. Core trust is trust in our life as it is as a trustworthy path to evolving in love, wisdom, and healing power. This is radical, nitty-gritty trust in bare-bones reality. Here our reliance is on the reliability of reality itself as right for us. This is because we trust it to grant us opportunities for growth and enlightened action.

Core trust, or surrendering to reality, is not only psychologically sane but also spiritually valuable. This follows when reality can be another word for the divine, the underlying evolutionary and sustaining force of the universe.

Core trust is an attitude of yes to the here-and-now predicaments of our lives as the perfect ingredients for building self-trust, increasing love, decreasing fear, and growing in wisdom and compassion. Our core trust is in how life unfolds, in the built-in synchronicity between events that come our way and opportunities for evolving. This means trusting that the universe may hurt but will not deliberately harm us. It may not satisfy, but it will fit our needs. Core trust means believing, with the same certainty with which we believe that the weather will change, that all that happens can ultimately be useful to our growth, can open paths on which we can advance in wisdom and love.

Sometimes that growth happens all by itself, and sometimes we are challenged to use skillful means to help it along. Our trust is core trust because it is actually trust in the *core of ourselves*. Built into our human personhood is a gift from the universe. *This gift is an ability, an inclination to make something good, growth-fostering, or useful out of anything that happens, no matter how painful or negative it is.* This is also a way of saying that the universe is ultimately friendly, helpful to and in favor of our evolving richly in love, wisdom, and healing power. Thus, nothing is fully negative, since anything can be passed through the life-trusting core of us and be transformed. As early as the Book of Genesis, this possibility was noticed by humans and the word *God* was used for "core": "What you intended for evil, God has turned into good" (Gen. 50:20).

The frightened or doubting ego picks a quarrel with life's givens, demanding its right to a perfect world, the one to which it believes itself entitled. So it attempts to revamp the shape reality takes. It does this by trying to gain control. Then fear of reality replaces trust in reality. For instance, we may not believe that this moment, this predicament, and the suffering it entails, offers just what we need to keep us growing. Core trust is an unconditional yes to the trustworthiness of any reality that comes our way to give us a chance to practice mindfulness and loving-kindness—that is, a chance to be enlightened. In core trust the unconditional yes fully flowers. It is no longer seen simply as an acceptance of reality. In core trust, our yes is not dualistic in any way. It is not "I surrender to this out there," but "I am now a yes, one with this experience." This is the full blooming of mindfulness, and it leads to a spiritual contentment.

Psychological work can help us too. Control is an unconditional no, a refusal to accept, a rejection of oneness with our predicament, an insistence on ego's ascendancy over any reality. But control does not have to kick in. As the ego becomes healthier, it is drawn to the possibility of *managing* in the world. This is the other side of the coin of control. We notice that some things can be changed by our reasonable effort, and we work on having the courage to change them for the better. We also notice that we need others' support and can ask for it respectfully. Thus, the healthy ego builds a sense of mastery as well as effective bonding: "I can take action for myself, and I can let my needs be known to others. These are resources that can lead to their fulfillment." This is healthy managing, having agency in the world and connecting effectively to others too. This is the positive side of what in the extreme is controlling, demanding, and manipulating to get our needs met.

Our need to control is actually not a need; it is panic that our needs will not be met unless we take full charge. Twelve-step programs emphasize the serenity prayer: "God grant me the serenity to accept the things I cannot change, the courage to change the things I can, and the wisdom to know the difference." If we are always seeking control, we do not seek the "wisdom to know the difference" between what can be changed and what cannot. This compulsion may have begun early in life when our caregivers did not meet our needs with the immediacy and accuracy we demanded. We began controlling when we noticed that the way life unfolds does not guarantee our safety and security. We may actually have been held and cared for most adequately in the realm of physical needs. But overall, when it came to attuning to our emotions and our other unique requirements, none of us was held or comforted enough. No holding environment was perfect. Some of us became controlling as a result of our panic about our needs not being met. Some of us became more adept at reasonable and effective ways of getting them met without having to be controlling.

Our need to be in full control arises from the compulsive push to be sure to get what we need—going all the way back to childhood. At some point, we gave up relying on others' responsiveness or on how the chips of life might fall. We despaired that our needs would be met in the normal course of events. We therefore insisted on having it our way. This fear-based controlling then became a permanent aspect of ourselves, who we turned out to be, our identity. Unfortunately, it moves us in the opposite direction of core trust.

Finding safety and security in the scared ego and its version of how life should be leads to a despair about our true powers. The reality is that needs are met or unmet, beyond our control, and *we have the power to survive in either circumstance.* In fact, cultivating the ability to survive any contingency is more valuable for our growth than getting what we want. The former shows us how to ask to have our needs met without having to manipulate. The reality is that we will survive best when we grow from our disappointments in others and trust that what we need will happen in any case. This takes core trust, both the antidote to despair and the freedom from the compulsion to control. Now we have found our authentic power, our capacity to deal with whatever life brings. When we realize at last that our ego is not omnipotent but puny in the face of the givens of life, we become more humble about ourselves.

At the same time, the extreme of total self-reliance reflects a mistrust of reality. We believe our ego to be the only game in town because we imagine that there is nothing reliable to trust beyond ourselves. We may feel that there is no support out there for us. This is not a reflection of reality but of the gap between our ego desires and our destiny—to keep receiving consciousness-increasing opportunities in the form of events and people.

The gap is the space between our ordinary personality, designed by the controlling ego, and our true wholeness, designed by the ongoing flow of reality. The gap feels as if we have no platform on which to stand unless we construct it, no safety net in which to land unless we weave it, no railing on which to lean unless we erect it. Our fall into this gap feels like being dropped. This makes us try even harder to get back in control. We fear a free fall into life's givens—though, actually, this would be our best lesson in flying.

When we realize at last that our ego is not omnipotent but powerless to topple the givens of life, we become more humble about ourselves. That is how our yes to reality becomes a spiritual advance. The yes of humility happens when we accept that things end and change rather than when we try to stop that from happening. We surrender to the natural flow of life rather than demand that our alternative agenda be followed. We notice that people are not loyal and loving all the time, but we choose to act lovingly and loyally toward them nonetheless. When suffering comes our way, we deal with it resiliently and thereby learn from it.

All this can sound like superstition without this important reminder: it is not that things happen *so that* we will learn from them. Our core trust is in the fact that things happen *and* we can learn from them. Core trust is in a visible opportunity, not in an invisible purpose. It is superstition to believe that everything will always turn out for the best. That is not wise trust but wishful thinking. Core trust is rather a confidence in ourselves that we will be able to make the best of whatever happens. Our trust is in our inner resources, not in our entitlement to have the world arrange itself to suit us. *All we can trust about what happens is that it will invariably give us a chance to grow.*

This is why core trust in reality does not make a case for predestination. It does not condone passivity in the face of evil. It does not decrease the value of engaging in action to avert wrongdoing, to fight injustice for ourselves and others. We look unceasingly for the courage to change what can be changed. At the same time, we fully accept the things that cannot be changed. This does not mean resignation but alignment to realities beyond our control.

Then we become agents of change without having to be in charge of how things change. We become effective in making a better life for ourselves and others without having to force anything. This sense of agency is the healthy alternative to control. Without core trust, we cannot find that alternative. We are forced to believe that if we let go of control, then everything will fall apart. Yet, paradoxically, we gain trust when we stop resisting the flow of life and inserting our agenda into it. We notice that we feel much less stress when we are agents of change where possible and acceptors of what is where necessary. We are not trying to constrain reality into the shape of our desires. We are no longer like the stepsisters of Cinderella, trying to force their feet into a slipper not meant for them.

Without core trust, we doubt that earth, just as it is, can be what Robert Frost called "the right place for love." Without core trust, we can't relax our grasp and let reality unfold as it needs to. Instead, we have to stay on guard, ever compelled to fix or change it, afraid it might not fulfill our desire for safety. With core trust, we gain confidence that nothing can happen to us that does not offer a fulfillment of our ineradicable yearning for wholeness. Thus, everything in our lives, whether from events or from people, is just what is needed for our unique story to be told. In other words, nothing can happen that is not already ours. Such confidence makes us fearless and makes the world a friendly place.

> *I say that we are wound*
> *With mercy round and round*
> *As if with air. . . .*
> —GERARD MANLEY HOPKINS, "THE BLESSED
> VIRGIN COMPARED TO THE AIR WE BREATHE"

The Supreme Attunement

> *The biggest risk: to trust that these conditions are all*
> *that I need to be myself.*
> —HAN HUNG, EIGHTH-CENTURY CHINESE POET

Trusting in reality, in life as it is, begins to make it clear that the world of events and our own true nature are one and the same. In medieval times, this was referred to as the *unus mundus,* the one world. The spiritual and material, the inner and outer, are all dimensions of one reality, the natural and the divine and the human the same in essence. How ironic that we humans were being asked all along to trust the world and not our ego, and yet trusting the world is really trusting our very selves anyway. Our need to change, fix, and rearrange reality was the sign of our distrust of how we were constructed as humans. Every hatch we battened down interfered with our full emergence.

The surrender to reality as benevolent does not mean we will not be hurt, only that somehow that hurt can help us be more present, can become an aid to evolution, can show us how to have more compassion. Our issues, our story, our conflicts, are thus all worthy vehicles to enlightenment. This is the implication of the Buddhist recommendation that we indulge in neither aversion nor attachment. Instead, we surrender to reality and flow with it, without preferences, trusting what happens as just the right recipe for letting the light through. We surrender when the five A's are applied to what is coming toward us here and now. We greet our unchangeable reality with attentiveness, acceptance, appreciation, affection, and, most of all, allowing.

Our surrender has led not to knuckling under or falling on our face but to taking it on the chin, "like lovers' pinches that hurt but are desired," as Shakespeare says. Now we see the real courage of the true self, so much more powerful than the bigshot ego. This does not mean that the ego is done for; it loves its new side-by-side position. It can finally relax and go off its demanding sentry duty. It can rest in the arms of reality. The resulting contented self is the equivalent of a holding environment, so we have found at last what the ego always wanted: safety and security within ourselves no matter what blow or embrace the world metes out.

Our core trust generates a calm abiding, a serenity that energizes. The opposite of being in control is resting secure and being alert to what comes next. Now we can enter any experience and go through it, bringing our security and sense of agency with us, even if we are afraid. The terror of uncertainty opens into spaciousness. We do not feel dropped but received. To open to reality is to turn toward it and to trust that it makes room for us in that very same moment. Dante shows us this trust in the *Purgatorio:* "The infinite goodness has such wide arms that it takes whatever turns to it."

All this happens as we let go of control and stay with whatever happens until it transforms. This is the supreme attunement, one we discover, not one we wait for from others, as we did in infancy. It is aligning ourselves to our true nature, our Buddha-nature, beyond ego, one and the same as the reality that faces us in any here and now. Our enlightened—Buddha— nature is always and already alive in us, transcending our personal limitations. Our spiritual practices and effort are meant to expose this enlightened nature in our daily life. Our essential-potential goodness and wisdom then become existential-actual. Here is an example: we are always and already intelligent, but our commitment to diligent study is required to activate that potential in specific ways. We have what it takes internally, but it comes alive only when we cooperate externally.

The past and future are mental constructs. Each time we return to the present, we feel a continuity with the time we did it before. Gradually, all those present moments link together, and it feels to us that only one continuous present is happening. That is why the accent in spiritual practices is on repeated return to the here and now. Such a position is also appealing to the natural inclination in us, going back to caveman times, when staying present was essential to survival.

A fascinating result of core trust is this: Our focus on and curiosity about our own life increase. Our *interest* in our suffering becomes greater than our need to find relief from it. Our fascination is with seeing what this particular suffering of ours is about and how it can serve us and others.

We grow in confidence when we realize that we have it in us to open ourselves to any human eventuality, even our sufferings. This is healthier for us than increasing our skill at evading or blunting the wallop of reality. We are no longer hot and bothered by our painful experiences but open to them. Indeed, liberation from the desire to control our pain is the other side of the coin of healing. This is respect for purely felt reality.

All our avoidances and add-ons were nothing but resistances, which now become revelations: "When I give up trying to direct the show and instead keep opening to how it unfolds,

I unfold. What makes a personal appearance is so much more interesting than the ego version of me. Imagine! I have spent my whole life rehearsing my minor role in the high school play when the lead in *Star Wars* was waiting for me."

The pure experience of life as it is appeals to our sense of power rather than to our sense of victimization. We no longer use our life events to lament our fate, embroider our story, or extend our ego control. We simply remain present to what happens and to how we feel rather than trying to gain an upper hand, the hand that the inflated ego plays so desperately and so cunningly.

Many synchronicities happen to me while writing a book. For example, the night after writing the section above, I saw the 1961 film *The Misfits*. To my pleasant surprise, I heard a simple and clear example of the point I am trying to make about our core trust in whatever happens. Montgomery Clift asked Marilyn Monroe, "What do you depend on?" Her answer: "The next thing that happens." This is a profound expression of trusting what unfolds, implying that we can have faith in reality as benevolent and evolving. Since this is just what we are meant to do too, our human task is simply to go with what is happening, to stay in the saddle in the direction the horse is going in, to attune to reality. The only caveat we might place on Marilyn's wisdom is that an openness to what comes along may mean a lack of discernment and loss of boundaries. This is the shadow side of trustful receptivity. Wisdom requires us to open to what happens *and* be discriminating about what we let in.

Finally, with all this recommending of harmony with reality, we cannot overlook or underestimate the creative powers in *disharmony* with it. Italian poet Eugenio Montale wrote, "I always felt total disharmony with reality and this disharmony has been the source of my inspiration." We who have been marginal rather than mainstream in life know that gift. But we also notice that the margin can be the leading edge—not necessarily the failure—of our fidelity to reality.

Practice

FIDELITY TO OURSELVES

Our inherent nature contains all the human possibilities of pain and pleasure. Each arises at different times, expecting to be greeted as equals at our threshold. When we stay with our feelings, they soon open into their opposites. For instance, "I feel lonely and separate. I go into the hole inside where I am insulated. That hole begins to become an opening, and then I reenter the world and feel a connection to it." This is the opposite of isolation. We give sovereignty to our experience. In the following practice, we apply all this to a specific situation.

At some time, you were lonely. Immediately, without conscious effort or choice, you probably took some inner or outer action. You thought or did something. For instance, you told yourself the story of how no one really wants to be with you, maybe even noticing evidence of that going all the way back to childhood. You thereby confirmed your habitual belief about yourself as a victim, someone unlovable or unworthy.

You may have felt anxiety or fear that things would get a lot worse if you just sat there and felt lonely. (Actually, the story and beliefs are what make that happen, not the loneliness itself.)

In a panic, you turned to an addictive behavior, or you called someone to gossip, or you turned on the TV to keep you company, or you ate something—or *did* whatever usually works to help you escape from your actual condition in the moment.

You can befriend the demon of loneliness—or any demon—
using a simple, but perhaps at first scary, practice:

1. Freeze-frame yourself: stay put as soon as any feeling or
   state of mind arises.
2. Allow yourself to feel your feelings, to stay with your
   experience, as fully as you can, for one more minute than
   you think you can stand.
3. Have a positive buffer lined up, something that is nurturant and has no story, belief, or addiction attached to it.
   For instance, take a walk in nature; read or write a poem;
   or if eating does it for you, make it something healthy—a
   tangerine, a cup of tea. These are enriching rather than
   escapist pastimes.
4. Then and only then, go to your usual buffers or distractions if you still want to.

Each time you simply let yourself be for that one more
moment, you make an exponential contribution to becoming
more comfortable with yourself, trusting of your feelings, friendly
to your immediate experience. *Eventually, it will be more interesting to stay with yourself than to use any buffer at all.* The story, the
beliefs, and the actions that are meant to reverse your experience become unnecessary and even amusing to you. You have
entered your reality rather than scampering away from it.

Then you will notice, with joy, that you trust the universe
and your trusty inner resources so much more. What began as
a feeling or predicament you thought you had to avoid at all
costs became a rich opportunity for practice and growth. We
can change our style from "getting rid of" to "working with."
Then we can experience not only loneliness but anything that
life brings because we are no longer caught in fear of it. The
demon has turned into an ally.

Saigyo, a Japanese Zen poet, lived in a shack as a hermit.
This is the poem he wrote after *being* there awhile:

> This place would be
> Unbearable
> If it weren't for the loneliness.

Four Reliable Directions

Our trust can move in four directions: we can trust ourselves,
others, reality, and a higher power. Put differently, the four
forms of trust are: self-trust, interpersonal trust, core trust
(trusting reality), and faith (trusting in a higher power). If one
or more directions of trust are omitted, then too much pressure
is put onto the others. For instance, if we can't trust people,
then we pressure ourselves unduly. The challenge is to access
all four vehicles of trust.

Trusting ourselves means that we trust our own body/mind as
a most suitable instrument for living in a psychologically and
spiritually healthy way. Self-trust is self-esteem. We know we
can trust ourselves with others when we can receive their trustworthiness with appreciation and handle their untrustworthiness without becoming destabilized and without retaliating
against them. This presumes equanimity, the ability to move
through mental states and life predicaments with a suppleness
of attitude and feeling. Equanimity is what reliability looks like
when it resides in ourselves. The commitment not to exact revenge is a result of our growth in spiritual consciousness through
our loving-kindness practice. That commitment is a sign that
we trust the wisdom in teachings that recommend nonviolence
as a path.

Trusting others happens when we believe that they have our best interests at heart. We trust that they will come through for us, stand by us, and be there for us when we need them. We believe they will not knowingly or purposely betray, disappoint, deceive, or hurt us. If they do, we trust ourselves to handle those experiences by grieving and attempting to reconcile if that is appropriate to the situation.

Trusting reality is confidence that whatever happens to us beyond our control is precisely what can provide the occasion for us to grow in our own unique way. This does not mean that we resign ourselves to injustice or that we become doormats, only that we align ourselves to what cannot be changed and look enthusiastically for its teaching. We trust reality when we believe that the universe is helping us evolve. Then circumstances and predicaments are not roadblocks but vehicles to our becoming people of character, depth, and compassion. The bumps and misfortunes of life are how that happens. Our accepting them without reserve is how we show our trust in reality as it is. Then we are ready to change what can be changed and know the difference too.

Trusting a higher power can mean belief in a personal God or in any force or spirit in nature or the universe that transcends ego and can be relied upon for grace and support. Trusting in Buddha-nature, the enlightened core of all of us, means trust that we have basic goodness, love, enlightened wisdom, and equanimity, that we believe these qualities are always within us potentially, always ready for actualization. Full activation of our potentials turns possibilities into powers. These become our inner resources as we face life, events, and people and all the challenges they present.

Surrendering to the will of God, as in "Thy will be done," is a religious version of core trust. Thus, trusting God is the same as trusting reality. In an interview with Frederick Sands shortly before his death, Carl Jung said, "God is the name by which I designate all things which cross my path violently and recklessly, all things which alter my plans and intentions, and change the course of my life, for better or for worse." In that sense, God and reality are the same. Core trust and trust in a higher power are essentially one.

We hear a similar view from contemporary theologian and monk Thomas Keating in his book *Open Mind, Open Heart:* "To pray without ceasing is to be aware of the divine presence all the time as *a spontaneous part of reality*" (italics mine). In this view, we trust in what happens to us as the way the divine unfolds and incarnates itself in daily life. God is then not an entity or a separate person but an immanent reality that is transcendent of ego. This is what can make the higher power within our "unsuspected inner resource," to use a term from Alcoholics Anonymous.

Trust in a higher power, from an adult perspective, is reliance on one immensely heartening belief: nothing that can happen to us can obstruct our path to finding meaning in the world or achieving our fulfillment as humans. This does not have to mean that there is predestination or intervention from above. It means that every predicament in our lives, in itself, offers us the possibility of evolving. No matter how threatening the forces of evil and hate may become, we can somehow break free from them, even when we find them in ourselves. Trust in a higher power means having confidence that no power on earth can hold us captive to hate or prohibit us from loving. Now we can see why adult and abiding faith is a challenge for so many of us. It requires that we take responsibility for activating our inescapable and ever-clamoring potentials. It is the opposite of stuckness, inability to launch, or fear of going on. Of course, part of faith is believing in an assisting and activating grace, and thus faith can give great hope.

Finally, we can summarize what we learned in earlier chapters and connect it with the four directions of trust:

In Childhood We Learn to Trust Because
These Five Elements Are Present

1. Bonding with trustworthy caregivers
2. Having our feelings and moods mirrored by them
3. Being attuned to the five A's (attention, acceptance, appreciation, affection, and allowing)
4. Finding a safe haven in someone with strength and wisdom when we feel threatened or confused
5. Finding a secure base in someone who models composure under stress

All five of these are provided to us reliably and in an inclusive, reassuring, flexible manner so that safety and security result.

These Same Five Qualities Will Characterize
Our Trust in Ourselves and Others

1. Feeling supported by bonding with trustworthy partners and friends
2. Having our feelings and moods mirrored by them
3. Being attuned to the five A's—and attuning to ourselves in those same ways
4. Finding a safe haven in our own strength and wisdom when we feel threatened or confused, especially in mindfulness and inner silence
5. Believing that we and others can be a secure base to one another and acting in accord with that confidence

These Qualities Will Also Be What Makes for Trust
in Reality and in a Transcendent Power

1. Feeling bonded to all beings in loving-kindness
2. Showing empathy and compassion to others and feeling those qualities come to us from powers beyond our ego
3. Attuning to and surrendering to the givens of life and feeling attuned to by powers beyond ourselves
4. Finding a safe haven in the strength and wisdom that flow from mindfulness and inner silence, especially in nature or in mystical experiences
5. Acting with virtue and integrity so that each of us can be trusted as a secure base for one another

Practice

USING OUR COMPASS OF TRUST

Check out your relationship to the four directions trust can take by drawing a compass, an image of a trusty tool for finding our way on a journey.

Place the words "I TRUST" in the center with a circle around it.

In the east position, write "MYSELF."

In the west position, write "OTHERS."

In the south position is "REALITY" or "WHATEVER HAPPENS" or "HOW LIFE UNFOLDS."

In the north position, use whatever word represents for you "GOD OR A HIGHER POWER."

Draw arrows from the center circle to each of the four points on the compass. Notice the combination, a horizontal plane for people and a vertical plane for powers that transcend our control.

Draw curved lines on the face of compass from north to east

to south to west and back to north. This symbolizes how all the resources of trust connect and aid one another. *The four directions of trust become our main inner resources. We fall back on them throughout our life cycle.*

Now think of your most recent concern or problem—or how you handle things ordinarily. Ask yourself how you could trust in each of the four directions when it comes to handling this issue (or handling life in general). Do this by responding to the four questions or suggestions below for each direction of trust. Let each of your responses start you on a train of thought and feeling that can show you how to trust more fully and more effectively in each of the four resources. See them as allies in your dealing with your present or any predicament. An ally is anyone or anything that aids you in evolving, that wants or urges you to succeed, that coaches you toward what is best for you, that supports your self-discovery, that is your assisting force regarding:

Self-trust

1. What resources do you find in your body/mind, and how could you use them more?
2. How well can you rely on yourself to take action when you face a challenge?
3. What qualities, skills, and virtues do you trust in yourself?
4. What commitment will you make to stay with this issue by first pausing to contemplate it and, when you are ready, to address it so that it can be resolved?

Interpersonal Trust

1. What kind of support will you ask for from your partner or close friend? (Asking for help is a way of learning to

trust. Support from others ends our insecurity about our own self-worth.)

2. What will you tell your family or friends so that they can be of help to you?

3. If people do not come through for you, what plan do you have for handling that disappointment?

4. If you fear or are embarrassed about asking for help, can you work on that by admitting your fear to yourself and, if possible, to your family or friends, feeling your fear fully, and then not being driven or stopped by the fear?

Core Trust

1. How can you say yes unconditionally to what is happening so that you can gain the serenity to accept what cannot be changed?

2. How can you say yes unconditionally to what is happening so that you can gain the courage to change what can be changed?

3. How can you say yes unconditionally to your inner wisdom so that you can tell the difference between what can and cannot be changed?

4. Make a commitment to continue looking for what helps you to trust that the universe keeps providing opportunities for growth and wisdom, that this problem can further your evolution, that from it can come greater self-esteem and love for others.

Trusting a Higher Power

1. If appropriate to your belief system, use devotion and prayer to build your personal connection to God or to a higher power.

2. Drop down into the heart place in yourself where there is an infallible source of unconditional love, wisdom, and healing power and then picture yourself bringing these three qualities to bear on the issue at hand.

3. Imagine angels, saints, or Buddhas representing love, wisdom, and healing attending you now and in every phase of the problem and its resolution. If these traditional images are not appropriate, use whatever works for you.

4. Ask for the grace of trusting the messages that come in the forms of synchronicity, dreams, intuitions, and in any other ways that seem to originate from a force beyond your own making.

Affirmations for Building Trust in All Directions

May I grow in trust in myself by granting myself attention, acceptance, appreciation, affection, and allowing.

May I grow in trust of others by asking for their support, appreciating their way of giving it, and not blaming or punishing them if they fail me.

May I grow in trust of my present predicament as a path to wholeness and higher spiritual consciousness by accepting my here-and-now situation with equanimity as well as with some sense of humor.

May I keep trusting graces from powers beyond my ego.

May I stay aware that these powers are everywhere and always with me.

May I feel how they guide, guard, comfort, and cheer me.

May I grow in steadfast faith that cosmic powers always and everywhere care about the evolution of all of us.

May I always be thankful for the graces that keep coming my way.

Now I am aware that the words "I will fear no evil for thou art with me" apply not only to a higher power. They apply to all four of my trusty resources:

"I will fear no evil for I am with me."
"I will fear no evil for others are with me."
"I will fear no evil for the universe is with me."

Extend the Affirmations into a Loving-kindness Practice

May what I go through in this crisis or concern be of help to all people everywhere who are suffering in the same way I am. May whatever progress I make be of service to them too.

May I trust that I will never lose my capacity to love no matter what happens to me, and may I always know that nothing is more important than that.

In this practice of recalling and joining with all people everywhere who suffer as we do, we no longer see our particular pain as unique to us. Our sense of comradeship leads to a yes to the given of universal suffering. This is what frees us from suffering as isolated victims rather than as humans among fellow humans.

We can also say that suffering is more than a given of life. It is a symptom of still being caught in dualistic thinking, in wanting something other than what's going on at each moment— that is, not living in the now. Once we let go into the moment, suffering becomes simply part of the experience of being alive— and no more than that.

8

Trust in Powers beyond Us

So far in this book we have explored in detail the nature of self-trust, interpersonal trust, and core trust. Now we turn to the question of trust in God, or a higher power. What does wise, mature trust in a higher power look like?

Faith is usually described as reliance on invisible sources of support. Faith is what trust looks like when it focuses on the transcendent.

To a great extent, religious trust is based on our experience of reliability from our original caregivers. In our preverbal times, when they came through for us and even seemed to know our needs before we did, we came to trust that there were mysterious and powerful sources of reliability in the world around us, working in our favor. It is then easy for us later to feel that the givens of life are not inimical. We have come to believe in trustworthy forces around us.

If our early experiences did not include reliability or were abusive, our sense of how the world works may be based on a reward and punishment model. This makes a fear-based religious view more likely in later life. We then try to be in control of life's givens rather than say yes to them. Fear and control make it impossible for us to have faith in the sense of trust that we are in good hands. Yet, an unconditional yes to trust grants us equanimity in the face of any ogre or in the jaws of any shark.

Our early life influences our moral consciousness, since that is directly proportional to the stability of our sense of self. An inner strength originating in childhood makes us morally robust. We are then able to resist immediate gratification for a higher value, to extend our love beyond our near and dear, to forgive and reconcile, to make amends for our failings, to stand up against injustice, to act with honesty and integrity, to take responsibility for our world. It follows that parents best help their children become morally upright when they build children's trust in themselves rather than scare them with threats of hell and punishment. Children who trust themselves become adults who vanquish evil rather than join or deny it.

In childhood, our mother's arms helped us trust in a person. The all-compassing merger we felt with her gave us a sense of transcendence *at the same time.* That equipped us with the possibility of believing in a personal and nurturant God, a transcendent parent. Father, as symbolic of another aspect of this omnipotent force, adds to our sense of protection. We will have trouble trusting a transcendent parent if we were not able to trust our own parents and other caregivers in childhood. Then we have work to do on ourselves before we can learn to trust others in intimate relationships or God / higher power / Buddha-nature in relation to us.

In any case, it is possible to have a belief in a transcendent, higher power without having faith in a literal God. Our transcendent force might be nature or our hope in humanity. That appreciation or trust makes us feel at home in the world, giving us a sense of safety and reassurance. Such confidence in the meaningfulness of the world can be the equivalent of trust in a personal divine presence behind it all. This is stated well in the Rogers and Hammerstein song from *Carousel:* "Walk on, walk on with hope in your heart, and you'll never walk alone." There is no mention of God in the song, but *hope is the equivalent of presence.*

It is understandable that humans over the centuries came to believe in and rely on a transcendent presence. Accompaniment is so important that we need an absolutely trustworthy friend, a totally reliable guardian, an ever- and everywhere-present comrade. Then we can walk on through any dark valley, even that of death, "for thou art with me." We still seek that accompaniment. We even carry the words *In God we trust* on the currency in our pockets!

At first perhaps that presence seemed to be a male Someone in the sky, but, as we evolved, our sense of the transcendent did not have to be personified. It could remain real but not literal. In childhood, religious symbols and literal religious beliefs can give us "transitional" comfort. Our faith usually begins with literal beliefs ("God lives up in the sky") and matures as we come to see their metaphorical nature.

Humans soon perceived the transcendent divine life as immanent, interior. This inner presence felt like a reliable source of support extending beyond us that we could trust. The numinous quality of the inner presence came through when we found loving-kindness and wisdom within us. Then we could see the transcendent presence as our own enlightened nature. The more we become aware of the wonders in this inner nature of ours, the more does it feel like a living, loving, and reliable presence. This fulfills our need for a trustworthiness that transcends human shortcomings, a wider power than the narrow ego.

Faith in the divine feminine has to do with honoring the earth, not a literal goddess. In the ancient pagan concept of the mother goddess, she both nurtures and devours. Trusting her is trusting that she will certainly comfort us but that she will also overwhelm our ego when necessary in order to awaken our inner enlightened nature. Mature spiritual consciousness means that we do not split her into the good mother and the bad mother. Instead, we integrate her opposite energies of accepting us with loving care and showing enough wrath to call our ego to account too. The divine feminine offers both comfort and challenge.

As we saw in the chapter on core trust, God can be thought of as a metaphor for the reality that visits us in the givens of life. Then trust is the unconditional yes to the way things are, a joining with what happens so that our sense of separateness is gone. This style of unconditional yes is the traditional "Thy will be done." In fully adult faith, that prayer is no longer dualistic. It has become: "I am one with thy will." In this view the believer is in continual touch with God, who keeps appearing in whatever happens. Every experience in life is then an epiphany. In Buddhism this might be expressed: Everything is the dharma, a teaching about how things really are or about the path to enlightenment.

Idealization happens when we see someone as perfect. We then believe that if we join with our idol, we too will be perfect—and complete. Our bond with the ideal parent, or spiritual teacher, thus makes us feel safe and secure. It becomes a launching pad. The positive results are that we form a clearer direction in life, gain a sense of personal stability, find our own purpose. When idealizing a teacher or religious authority becomes a permanent attachment, as happens in a cult, it has negative consequences. We cannot fulfill our developmental task of independence and creative thinking.

Within a formal religion, some teachers from our childhood may have taken advantage of our trust in them. They may have imprinted us with repressive injunctions that exploited and inhibited us. These indoctrinations are difficult to unseat because they entered our minds within a bond of total trust. That bond usually grants a long "shelf life" to what we were taught. We easily see, as we become more mature, how some spiritual teachers were grounded in fear and psychologically off base. But their self-negating teachings may remain in us because they have sunk into the unfathomable depths of our unconscious. It is hard to fish out the critters all the way down on the ocean floor. Our work is to clear ourselves of superstition and fear-based beliefs and to let go of resentment of teachers who were themselves sadly benighted.

If we have done things we are not proud of, we might imagine that we remain guilty—and punishable—all our lives. This is saying that not even God has the power to forgive us. We believe we have to be punished, maybe even after death. Fear of hell is the opposite of trust in God. Hell is a way of saying that God is an eternal torturer who has not evolved as far as heroic humans have, not yet found the power of nonviolent resistance to evil. That God is a metaphor for the vengeful entitled ego, not for unconditional love. A God of universal and unconditional love does not appeal to the ego, because that means no guarantee of retaliation, which is the ego's favorite sport. Even the gifts of grace in our lives may irritate the arrogant ego. Our ego feels humiliated by the whole idea of grace, since it is another unwelcome sign of its limited powers. Trust in a higher power includes believing that we are given the grace of forgiveness. Then self-forgiveness makes it possible to believe in the ultimate goodness in all beings. Thus, forgiving ourselves is a spiritual practice.

Finally, in childhood, imagination is a necessary ability in making sense of our world. Imagination can be harmful if it becomes more reliable than evidence. Faith is an accomplishment of the imagination, so it can have a positive impact on our spiritual creativity. Imagination is our most fundamental religious power, since we can picture and believe in something for which there is no tangible proof. How ironic that some religions abbreviate and stunt our imaginations by a dogmatism that scares us away from thinking outside the box.

It is our wonderful power of imagination that makes it possible to believe in love when we see only hate, in wisdom when we see only ignorance, in healing when we see only hurt, in life when we see only death. Thus, healthy faith is the culmination of what imagination can do. This is not imagination in the sense of a pirate's fantasies about buried treasure but a spiritually conscious adult's recognition of hidden riches in ourselves, in others, in reality, and in powers beyond our ego.

> *Our basic core of goodness is our true self. . . . The acceptance of our basic goodness is a quantum leap in our spiritual journey. God and our true self are not separate. Though we are not God, God and our true self are the same thing.*
>
> —THOMAS KEATING,
> *OPEN MIND, OPEN HEART*

Our Longing for Meaning

> *Self-actualization, if made an end in itself, contradicts the self-transcendent quality of human existence. . . . Only to the extent to which man fulfills a meaning out there in the world, does he fulfill himself.*
>
> —VIKTOR FRANKL,
> *THE UNHEARD CRY FOR MEANING*

We look high and low for meaning. This is directly related to trust, because we are looking for something to rely on. Yet, we notice that life experiences do not come with handy explanations or guarantees. We seek meanings in psychology, in religion, in ourselves. We then hope that our meanings reflect reality. Are we imposing meanings on neutral realities, or are we discovering a meaningful world?

Without experience, we are stuck with concepts and constructs, our interpretations of ideas that have come our way. We are then two steps removed from bare-bones reality. In any case, the adult journey is a labyrinthine path. It shows us over and over that there is no neat final summation, no perfectly orderly system, no unquestionable elucidation of what life is about. Instead, meanings and purposes are up in the air most of the time, though we are blessed with occasional moments in which all seems right with the world and with us.

When we begin in mindfulness, being faithful to our experience in the here and now, the question of meaning is not expected to be answered in any permanent way. We experience meaningful moments, feel meaningful emotions, see and touch things that take on special meaning to us. A once-and-for-all, objective, ultimate meaning becomes irrelevant and unnecessary. Our need for final explanations vanishes. We are content with provisional meanings, as we are with provisional trust.

We all naturally seek to reduce confusion and uncertainty. Traditional religion boldly presents a clear-cut explanation of life, its meaning, and its purpose. It offers a secure refuge from the conundrums and confusions that face us in adult life. In a dominating religion, we may be asked for blind obedience and the surrender of our independence, both in thought and in moral choices. In a spiritually facilitating religion—the one that will be appealing to adults—we may be assisted in finding personal solutions within a context of shared meaning. Our authorization then comes from within.

When did our need to trust a tidy view of the universe begin? By age three we insist on a clear description of life and the world. We ask our parents how we were made, why the sky is blue, and endless other "whys" and "hows." A fully consistent, intelligible set of answers is appropriate in childhood. To grow up is to let go of demanding, or even needing, such clarity, consistency, and certainty.

As adults, we are content with some confusion, any number of blurred lines, unanswerable questions, an ever-increasing series of riddles. We have even noticed that if we want to learn more about life and explore our world, certainties become obstructions. When all is clear, we are deprived of the ability to accept the given of uncertainty. When the wonder-studded journey becomes satisfactory without the crystal clear directions, we are more intrepid bushwhackers. Landmarks become unnecessary.

Tolerating ambivalence, ambiguity, and uncertainty is a major signpost in adult development. Notice that this reflects perfectly what happens as we grow in trust: as children, we need absolute reliability; as adults, we are reconciled to the wider spectrum of human trustworthiness and untrustworthiness.

The spirituality of trust has a heuristic quality, searching not to find the final roomful of possessions but only to find new doorways. This means an ever more opening search rather than a closing answer. It is about seeking rather than being told what we are supposed to find. This is trusting in the most positive features of our postmodern view, which encourages liberality in ideas, individual autonomy, egalitarianism in relationships, relativism about beliefs, and a questioning of authority.

*Mature religious sentiment is integrative in the sense
of encouraging the individual to face complex problems. . . . without reducing their complexity.*

—Gordon W. Allport,
The Individual and His Religion

Buddhist Paths to Adult Trust

*The religion of the future will be a cosmic religion.
It should transcend a personal God and avoid dogma
and theology. . . . It should be based on a religious sense
arising from the experience of all things natural and
spiritual as a meaningful unity. Buddhism answers
this description.*

—attributed to Albert Einstein

Most Buddhist traditions are nontheistic, nontranscendent, in
the sense that there is no divine creator or omniscient, omnipotent being who oversees the universe or promises salva-
tion from it. The Tibetan tradition of Buddhism includes
many deities, but these are ultimately understood as personifi-
cations of our own far-reaching potentials and opportunities
for gaining wisdom. For instance, there are wrathful deities
who may attempt to obstruct us on the path to enlightenment.
They are not enemies, only stern teachers who show us how to
fight ignorance. Deities are not persons, but when they are de-
picted as persons, we are more likely to take notice of them,
the principle that makes iconography and devotion so useful
in spirituality.

The deities are visualized as aspects of the essential Buddha-
nature in all of us. They are not gods in the dualistic sense but
articulations of the many kinds of godliness in us. Godliness is

enlightened nature, somewhat analogous in Buddhism to a higher power.

In traditional religion, the source of grace and human wholeness is from God, usually through sacred rituals. In the Buddhist perspective, all we need is already and always in us. Rituals are not purveyors of grace from God, only enactments of the grace-filled Buddha-nature within us. The challenge is then to resist our monkey mind / ego when it works against our true nature. Mindfulness is a resource for that.

Faith from the Buddhist perspective is not belief without evidence. It is trust in our own experience. In discussing the Buddhist notion of faith, Sharon Salzberg, in *Faith: Trusting Your Own Deepest Experience,* says that its essence "lies in trusting ourselves to discover the deepest truths on which we can rely." Such trust is the opposite of the need to be obedient to a dogmatic authority. It is also a freedom from being sure about the ultimate questions or having a pat answer to life's enigmas. Her definition of faith reflects that of Teilhard de Chardin in *How I Believe:* "The only reason that can decide me to adhere to a religion must . . . consist in the harmony of a higher order which exists between that religion and the individual creed to which the natural evolution of my faith has led me."

Thus, an adult learns to trust in what arises from the depths of her inner life. She does not feel compelled to adhere to the orthodox perspectives of established religious authority or to New Age shibboleths. They have to match or reflect her own experience. She does not give up her discerning intelligence for the safety and security that come from blind faith. She has organismic trust in herself—that is, a trust in her body/mind as always and already enlightened. Our trust in our Buddha-nature is our trust in ourselves.

Such faith is a spirit of imaginative curiosity that lets questions bother us and it is all right with us. It is toleration for inquiry without final solutions, a satisfaction with metaphor and mystery. Indeed, an enlightened person is happy to have no definite or reliable place to stand that will be suitable for all occasions. His address is a movable feast. He has given up any craving for safety and security. Openness is his favorite resort.

Faith, according to Zen master Shunryu Suzuki, rests not in any person or list of beliefs but in being supported by something neither material nor spiritual: "This is our fully extended body which is the universe." Thus, the forces of nature can also represent a power that is transcendent of ourselves and ever upholds us.

The faith that has to be sure that there is a God who will come through for us or a heaven waiting for us is egoic faith—that is, a faith based on the need for assurances and entitlements. True faith happens when we trust without having to be certain about secure assistance, though we are open to it always. This is how faith differs from ordinary trust. *Our adult trust is provisional, based on what the record shows. Our faith is unconditional trust no matter what the record shows.*

In any case, a trust in God, in any adult religious tradition, is not an insurance policy that guarantees that God will exempt us from suffering. It is rather the inner assurance that no matter how much we suffer or how unjustly the world treats us, our capacity to love will remain intact. This is another way of saying that our unconditional trust is in inner inviolable goodness.

Our Buddha-nature remains untarnished and unaffected by any of our mistakes. It can be hijacked when we are hostages to our dramas, yet it remains indelibly in us, recoverable in mindfulness, only a breath away. This is why not even "what the record shows" can matter totally because we can always activate the trustworthiness inside us—and so can everyone else.

In traditional religion, one can also trust by believing that

God is personal and will share in our suffering. Faith then is in the companionship/presence of God. We feel what happens to us with God feeling it with us. "For thou art with me" is faith as trust.

As we saw above, the first truth in Buddhism implies that nothing can be fully trusted, let alone clung to. We are enlightened when we are lightened of the burden of making gods out of our desires and attachments. To expect the unsatisfactory to satisfy us is suffering. To expect the unreliable to be reliable is suffering. Buddhism offers an adult program and, at the same time, does include trust. That trust is in what are called the three refuges: the Buddha, the dharma, and the sangha.

The Buddha is the enlightened potential in ourselves and, collectively, in all beings. Taking refuge in the Buddha means taking refuge in the accessibility of enlightenment from within ourselves in this and in any moment, in this and in any predicament.

The dharma is the Buddhist teachings. Taking refuge in the dharma means trusting the practices it offers as reliable and skillful means on the path to enlightenment. Our trust is shown by the seriousness of our commitment to the practices, especially mindfulness and loving-kindness.

The sangha is the community of practitioners who follow the teachings. Taking refuge in the sangha means taking refuge in the power of comradeship between us and other practitioners. This includes compassion for those who struggle as we do in the challenge of letting go of fear and craving, the sources of suffering. We hope for the same compassion from them toward us.

The Buddha also represents direct experience rather than false refuge in ego mind-sets. The dharma is learning from that experience. The sangha is the ongoing relationships that arise from it.

All three refuges require faith. It takes faith to believe that all beings have basic goodness, a Buddha-nature. It takes faith to accept that letting go of attachment and following precepts of loving-kindness leads to true liberation. It takes faith to join with others in our practice and then to trust them.

When we are beset with doubt, we can practice in the Buddhist tantric style. This means taking our doubt not as a deal-breaker but as *something to work with,* a valuable opportunity for the entry of more light into our lives. The transcendent More in traditional religion can also refer to more light, enlightenment. We are lightened of the load of ego: fears never done with and desires never satisfied.

Refuges refer to reliance. In some traditions of Buddhism, there are no refuges. Our practice becomes living our lives with nothing to lean on. There is no-thing to fall back on. This can certainly challenge or strengthen our skill at forming core trust.

Buddha used the metaphor of a raft to explain how to use his teachings. It ferries us across the river of confusion, but then we leave it behind as we enter the jungle of daily life. Applying this to any traditional religious teaching, we can affirm that we do not cling to a creed, only use it to move us along on our journey. The teachings are transmitted from teacher to teacher and from generation to generation. In such ancestral faith, we believe what the ancients believe, not in them but with them. Trust is thus collective, not simply personal. This is how we know it can be appealing to the whole person.

The reliability of Buddha-nature, our inner ineradicable enlightened being, is the source of our cheerfulness about ourselves and humanity. It is the truly spiritual foundation of trust. We can trust access to a pure experience of the here and now, unhindered by distractions, with no detours from reality. We can trust that we can act with loving-kindness, no matter what others may do to us. We can trust that we can refrain from inflicting extra pain on ourselves, no matter how deeply we are mired in it. We can trust that we live in an ever-evolving universe, no matter how negatively things seem to be turning out so far. What a joy to have forms of trust such as those.

Trusting the Buddha-nature of others means that we never give up on them. We always know that they can find the enlightened path, that they have love inside them, that they can move out of their ego into a wider and higher way of living. This is why retaliation is never appropriate and loving-kindness always is. Our loving-kindness practice helps us allow others not to come through for us as we want, to stay over there away from us rather than over here with us, not always to fulfill our needs, sometimes to reject us altogether. Yet, we trust ourselves to receive their goodness if they show it and not turn against them when they do not. That is how spiritual trust finally becomes so victorious that it claims under the banner of love every territory over which the neurotic ego had held sway.

We maintain our healthy ego as we eliminate its neurotic tendencies one by one—for example, fear, judgment, preference, aggression, craving, control, comparison. Then we have what the Buddhist teacher Chögyam Trungpa referred to as "brilliant sanity," the qualities of spaciousness, clarity, and compassion. We are empty of ego as the sky is, fully open but containing birds, clouds, and rainbows too. In other words, there is still room for all the events and people in our lives while we are free of ego. Compassion is transcendent in its direction since it leads us away from ourselves and toward others. Our spiritual work is not then to abandon the world but to share ourselves in and for it. That is the way in fact.

Trust in the Higher Self

We know that the human psyche has both individual and collective aspects. We are unique in personality, alike in ancestry. We gain knowledge of ourselves when we look into the collective sources of religion, the myths, symbols, and images that have appealed to humanity from ancient times. We thereby grow not only from our own experience but from that of our forebears, who, like us, sought meaning in life and found it in imaginative ways. This is how the saints and sages we admire can help us. They point to goals and destinies that are more magnificent—and outrageous—than those we might have imagined possible for humans to achieve.

The *Self* with a capital *S* is Carl Jung's term for our mostly unconscious collective human identity beyond our individual ego. The Self is not an entity but rather a field that transcends any single personal identity while also being the animating force of every person. Likewise, it is the same as the energy of the whole universe. The Bhagavad Gita states it: "My higher nature is the life force that sustains the universe." This same Self, our "higher nature," can be what many people understand as God, or a higher power.

Our ego is our self with a small *s*. This is our personality, with its unique ways of thinking and feeling. Our ego, unlike the Self, is defined by our roles or behaviors and is subject to fear and desire. The ego can be healthy, helping us fulfill our goals in life. It can also become distracted in addictive and fearful ways and become a vehicle of suffering.

Our full identity is both ego and Self. The ego is born at birth and dies at death. The Self is unborn and undying. The ego is unique in each person. The Self is the same in all of us. The ego is in our body/mind. Our body/mind is in the Self.

The ego can be understood by psychology. The Self is a mystery. It does not yield to a description since it is not an "it," not a separate thing in a world of separate things, but the life force, the source of every "it."

We have noticed that the positive qualities of the Self are exactly the same ones used to describe God, Buddha, and the saints—love, wisdom, and healing power. We participate in the Self when we experience an epiphany moment of unconditional love, exceptional wisdom, and unusual healing. A commitment to live in accord with those three gifts is what is meant by wholeness.

For Carl Jung, our longing for wholeness *is* our spiritual instinct. Spirituality is commitment to enacting wholeness. We have then rounded out our life with the qualities of the transcendent. This will feel like the culmination and fulfillment of our human journey, incarnating the divine on earth.

The divine presence, in the Jungian view, is in the deep Self, the unconscious. Thus, Jung wrote, "We depend upon the unconscious psyche or 'the grace of God'—names make no difference." The words *depend upon* are synonymous with *trust*. To trust the divine is to trust our higher Self.

> Whenever our *love* becomes unconditional, we know that has happened by grace from a higher power than ego can manage or conjure. That moment of unconditional-love-through-grace becomes our felt sense of the divine.
>
> Whenever our *wisdom* is greater than our minds could reach unaided, a gift of grace, we experience a felt sense of the divine, since God is considered to be eternal wisdom.
>
> Whenever our ability to *heal* and reconcile, rather than retaliate and divide, becomes greater than is usual for us, we have a felt sense of the divine, since the divine life is about universal reconciliation and compassion.

All three instances are incarnational moments. This means that the transcendent divine, immanent in us, enters time and space. All three are unconjured and uncontrolled by us. We have a sense of something larger than we have ever been, and it is coming through us.

Carl Jung, in his interview with Frederick Sands, said, "One of the most important qualities of the human soul is its religious function, enabling man to come to peace with himself through understanding the superior force within him." In most religions, there is a belief in the goodness in all people, untarnished by anything they have done. Quakers speak of "that of God in everyone." In Christian tradition, we also hear of Christ consciousness, of an indwelling Spirit. In Hinduism, this is the divine spark in all beings. In Buddhism, it is said that everyone and everything has an enlightened, wise, and compassionate nature—a Buddha-nature. Jung calls the higher Self the God archetype in every person.

These are all ways of saying that everything is then More than it appears to be and that all of us are essentially good, though existentially, in daily life, we might not always choose to act that way. Yet, we know that being loved makes us feel good and leads to our wanting to be loving. Scientific studies have shown that compassion increases our immune response, making us healthier. These are our best indicators that goodness resides in us and is meant to be acted upon.

In the Jungian view, when ego and Self work together, we are "individuated." The ego/Self axis is an affiliation of our individual ego with the higher universal Self. This happens when the inflated ego, with its inclination toward fear, ignorance, and division, surrenders itself to the purposes of the higher Self. Then the fear becomes love, the ignorance becomes wisdom, and the division becomes reconciliation and healing.

The ego is thus not meant to be destroyed but simply redirected. We bridle our ego as we do a horse so it can better serve its purpose. This process involves letting go of ego entitlement and self-centeredness. Instead, our focus becomes showing unconditional love and acting with compassion and wisdom as we contribute to the healing and evolution of the world. Spiritual practices help us forge that ego/Self bond. Thus, individuation reaches its climax when our personal integration and our universal connectedness become one and the same experience. This is why psychological health and spiritual health are ultimately the same.

As we lighten ourselves of the heavy wardrobe of ego, we automatically let the light of spiritual awareness in, since our ego is no longer blocking it out. The ego has now become a path to the light, not a roadblock in the way of it. We can trust that alongside the confusions of ego are indeed goodness, wise qualities, enlightened ways of behaving.

The Self always urges us toward wholeness. Thus, all events, both those felt to be positive and those felt to be negative, are grist for the mill of committing ourselves to the ongoing project of keeping our ego aligned to the Self. This is why core trust is so appropriate to our advance toward wholeness: "the almost irresistible compulsion and urge to become what one is," as Jung says. For him, wholeness was the essence of spirituality. It is an urge within us as strong as that of survival or sex.

Who we are at our best is bliss, love, and goodness. A religion and spirituality that are healthy for us will facilitate and encourage a life that is bursting with those three qualities. It will not be about repressing liveliness but enjoying it. As Thomas Merton wrote in *Love and Living,* "It is precisely in the spirit of celebration, gratitude, and joy that true purity is found."

In this chapter, we have been exploring the idea of trust in a higher power. We have examined contributions from religion, spirituality, Buddhism, and Jungian thought. Each offers its own spin on the meaning of life in the form of ideas, practices, and principles. We would not be fair to our topic if we did not add one point: We may choose not to follow any of these ready-made paths. We may already have or be finding our own unique path. This is always a totally valid, not to mention exciting and courageous, option.

Practice

AWAKENING AT MANY LEVELS

We can now distinguish our healthy ego from our neurotic ego and, further, from our spiritually awakened ego. Our healthy ego makes us functional in the world by choosing what helps us fulfill our life goals, including having healthy relationships. Our neurotic ego, as we saw earlier, is the FACE we are trying to save: fear, attachment, control, and entitlement. Our spiritually awakened ego is in an axis with the Self and has found ways to love unconditionally and universally, live wisely, and bring healing/reconciliation to the world. This chart helps us see the three at a glance:

The Healthy Ego	*The Neurotic Ego*	*The Spiritually Awakened Ego*
Psychological work is required to build it.	*A spiritual commitment is required to transform it.*	*Spiritual practice is required to develop it.*
Intelligent caution and less and less concern about how others judge us	Fear that others might not like us	Loving-kindness
Self-trust and self-esteem	Attachment to being right and inability to apologize	Wisdom and openness

The Healthy Ego (contd.)	The Neurotic Ego (contd.)	The Spiritually Awakened Ego (contd.)
Coping and managing effectively both as an individual and in relationships	Control of others and of events	Unconditional yes to people as they are and to life unfolding as it does
Standing up for our rights but without retaliation and accepting the givens of life with appropriate feelings but without complaint or blame	Entitlement to be first, to be respected by everyone, to be irresponsible without having to make amends, to take revenge, and to be exempt from the givens of life	"Live and let live" attitude and genuine caring about how to reconcile and forgive
These are abilities.	*These are disabilities.*	*These are graces.*
Result: sanity	*Result: worldly success or constant disappointment*	*Result: sanctity*

Work with this chart by asking yourself where your own patterns of thought, behavior, and relationship show up on this grid.

Most psychology and psychotherapy focuses on building a healthy ego. It usually does not focus on high ideals or the transformation of the individual and of the species. It concentrates on how the individual can become healthy enough to achieve personal serenity and happiness. Such a minimalist view does not expect enough from us ever-evolving and continually surprising humans. We can be much more than what is described in the Psych 101 textbook.

An example of how psychological work and spiritual awakening can coalesce is in the twelve-step programs of recovery from addiction. All the trusty tools of psychology cannot achieve sobriety and recovery. As Carl Jung suggested to Bill Wilson, the founder of Alcoholics Anonymous, what is required is a spiritual program. This means:

Acknowledgment of the powerlessness of ego
Grace from a higher power than ego
Fellowship with other people who support us on the path

Reminding ourselves of what we explored in the section above on Buddhism, the first is the equivalent of the Buddha, the second of the dharma, the third of the sangha—foundations of trust. A practice is to look at how you use each of these three sources of trust in your daily life:

How do you rely on your inner potentials for universal and unconditional love, the wisdom of the ages, and healing power?
How often do you ask for grace from powers beyond yourself?
How often do you give thanks when grace comes your way?
How close are you to mentors and supportive friends or to a group that assists you in finding the strength you need to take your next step?

Epilogue

Trust in Grace-full Coincidence

Throughout this book, we have alluded to synchronicity, the archetype of the assisting force—a grace—that shows itself in meaningful coincidences we could never bring about on our own. We can trust the opportunities that come to us in such synchronous moments. Perhaps our attention to what happens naturally and beyond our control gives us pointers about where our evolution can proceed most profitably. This is not superstition but trust in how the unconscious, and other powers beyond our ego, figures into knowing and activating our full selves. Synchronicity can always be relied on to direct us to spiritual practices. This follows from their purpose: Spiritual practices are not performed so that we can become enlightened. They are what we do because we are already innately enlightened in our deepest being. Spiritual practices express and incarnate that awesome fact.

I would like to close with a striking personal example of a grace of synchronicity that happened just as I was nearing the end of writing this book. This exceptional event helped me psychologically and simultaneously showed me the power of the loving-kindness practice.

My half brother called me from Connecticut to tell me that, completely by chance, a friend of his had shown him a photo of my father from 1932, at his eighth-grade graduation. This friend had no idea that my father was in this photo. He was showing my brother a photo of his own father's eighth-grade graduation, and my brother recognized my father in it, standing right beside his friend's father. (The list of names on the back of this photo confirmed that it was indeed my father.)

My brother sent me a copy of the photo, which I greatly appreciated. I stared at it with many thoughts and realized that only eight years later, this boy in the photo would be my dad, and ten years later he would be gone. (My parents divorced when I was two, and my father moved away for good.) I also noticed that no particular feeling came up for me in all this, which was unusual for me.

On the Sunday morning after receiving the photo, I went to hear the weekly dharma talk at Green Gulch Farm, a Zen community in Marin County in northern California. I had arrived early, so I took the opportunity to lie on the grass in the sun. Nearby was a play area, and I could hear the cries and shrieks of children but no articulation of their words. Suddenly, one clear sentence came sailing over the field into my ear, as if it were meant just for me, and was followed immediately again by the inarticulate clamor. A small boy seemed to be responding to a question by a playmate. His exact words, pronounced with great feeling, burned into me: "I have a daddy, but he lives far, far away, in San Diego." (That is the southerly California city farthest from Marin.)

Tears began to stream down my face. I felt the pain of loss in the child's voice so keenly. I thought of my own dad, who lived far from me for my entire childhood. Then I thought of how many children have had that experience of distance when parents divorce. I remember saying to myself, "Dads do that sometimes."

I kept crying copiously and made sure not to interrupt my experience by getting up from the grass or wiping my eyes. I knew it was important to let this crying happen and to let it go where it needed to go. Soon, keening sounds came up from me, who knows from how far down. I remained open to the experience, grateful for the unexpected and unplanned opportunity to exhume these long-entombed feelings. I made no attempt to stop the tears or sounds by trying to figure them out—my familiar and distracting tendency.

Only later did I contemplate and try to understand what had happened to me. I realized the connection with the photo. I had looked at it without grief for the father-son relationship I missed out on. The unshed tears waited for their chance to flow so that I could let go of a little more of the grief I hold inside. The meaningful coincidence of my hearing the boy I never saw—just what I needed for an opening to happen in me. *Does the universe position things so carefully that our hearts can open at just the right time? Is it that friendly?*

This experience was also a concrete example of the power of a commitment to loving-kindness practice: I had moved seamlessly and without effort from the boy's pain to my pain to all children's pain. That shift from personal to universal compassion happens in us as the direct result of the loving-kindness practice. What a stunning example of how our spiritual practices operate hand in glove with our psychological work.

That synchronicity fit with all the other synchronicities that led to it: my brother's having a friend who was my father's classmate, his recognizing my father, my receiving a copy of the photo before Sunday, my coming early to the talk so I would have time to lie down, a sunny day to make lying on the grass appealing, the grass being near the playground, the privacy to cry and keen, the boy with a story like mine, his single sentence being the only one that came through clearly—this was my true dharma talk that day.

What mysterious power makes it all come together just like that? How can we—you, the boy who so poignantly repeated the word *far,* and I—ever doubt that we can dare to trust?

> *We all have moments when the universal life seems to wrap us round with friendliness.*
>
> —WILLIAM JAMES,
> *THE VARIETIES OF RELIGIOUS EXPERIENCE*

About the Author

David Richo, PhD, MFT, is a workshop leader and psychotherapist in Santa Barbara and San Francisco, California, whose work combines Jungian and Buddhist perspectives. He has written more than twelve books on psychological and spiritual growth. For more information, including events and audio programs, visit http://davericho.com.

Books and Audio

BY DAVID RICHO

How to Be an Adult in Love: Letting Love in Safely and Showing It Recklessly (Shambhala Publications, 2013)

Embracing the Shadow: Discovering the Hidden Riches in Our Relationships (Shambhala Audio, 2013)

Coming Home to Who You Are: Discovering Your Natural Capacity for Love, Integrity, and Compassion (Shambhala Publications, 2012)

Daring to Trust: Opening Ourselves to Real Love and Intimacy (Shambhala Publications, 2010)

Being True to Life: Poetic Paths to Personal Growth (Shambhala Publications, 2009)

Making Love Last: How to Sustain Intimacy and Nurture Genuine Connection (Shambhala Audio, 2008)

Wisdom's Way: Quotations for Contemplation (Human Development Books, 2008)

When the Past Is Present: Healing the Emotional Wounds That Sabotage Our Relationships (Shambhala Publications, 2008)

The Power of Coincidence: How Life Shows Us What We Need to Know (Shambhala Publications, 2007)

The Sacred Heart of the World: Restoring Mystical Devotion to Our Spiritual Life (Paulist Press, 2007)

Mary Within Us: A Jungian Contemplation of Her Titles and Powers (Human Development Books, 2007)

(continued on next page)

The Five Things We Cannot Change: And the Happiness We Find by Embracing Them (Shambhala Publications, 2005)

How to Be an Adult in Relationships: The Five Keys to Mindful Loving (Shambhala Publications, 2002), also available as an audiobook (Shambhala Audio, 2013)

Shadow Dance: Liberating the Power and Creativity of Your Dark Side (Shambhala Publications, 1999)

When Love Meets Fear: How to Become Defense-less and Resource-full (Paulist Press, 1997)

How to Be an Adult: A Handbook for Psychological and Spiritual Integration (Paulist Press, 1991)